Windows on the Past
The Cultural Heritage
Hancock C

For Sharon,
Thank you for
hosting our Christmas
luncheon!
Barbara Williams Dunlap
December 9, 2010

Windows on the Past
The Cultural Heritage of Vardy, Hancock County, Tennessee

by
DruAnna Williams Overbay

MERCER
UNIVERSITY PRESS

ISBN 0-86554-950-8   MUP/P299

Windows on the Past:
The Cultural Heritage of Vardy, Hancock County, Tennessee
Copyright ©2005
Mercer University Press, Macon, Georgia USA
Printed in the United States of America
First edition, July 2005

The paper used in this publication meets the minimum requirements
of American National Standard for Information Sciences—
Permanence of Paper for Printed Library Materials,
ANSI Z39.48-1984.

Library of Congress Cataloging-in-Publication Data

Overbay, DruAnna Williams, 1942– .
　　Windows on the past : the cultural heritage of Vardy, Hancock County,
Tennessee / DruAnna Williams Overbay. — 1st ed.
　　p.　cm.
　　Includes bibliographical references and index.
　　ISBN-13: 978-0-86554-950-0 (pbk. : alk. paper)
　　ISBN-10: 0-86554-950-8 (pbk. : alk. paper)
　　1. Oral history. 2. Vardy (Tenn.)—History. 3. Vardy (Tenn.)—Social
life and customs.　I. Title.
　　F444.V37O94 2005
　　976.8'946—dc22

　　　　　　　　　　　　　　　　　　　　　　　　　2005028636

Contents

Dedication

This book is dedicated to
the memory of Vardy Community Center
spiritual leaders, staff and students,

and especially to my mother.

Acknowledgments

Sitting amid scattered manuscripts while listening again to the Vardy Oral Histories tapes during Christmas 2004, I wonder where does one begin in mentioning all of those individuals who have contributed to the writing of this book? The first person I must thank is my husband Fred who has supported me unconditionally during all of my endeavors to "set the record straight" about my Melungeon heritage. Certainly my parents Alyce and Drew Williams must be remembered, for they knew that one day I would write our stories. They gave me hundreds of photographs, letters, manuscripts, church and school records, newspaper clippings, and magazine articles, preparing me for this moment. I really think my mom wanted me to be the spokesperson for her family despite her anger when hearing the word "Melungeon" mentioned. She finally relented in 1981, and began writing her own memories for me to find after her death.

This book would not have been possible without the generous help of a number of individuals and organizations dedicated to the preservation of the cultural heritage of Vardy in Hancock County, Tennessee. The first organization I wish to thank is Humanities Tennessee for its support and cooperation in the completion of the Vardy Oral Histories Project for which the Vardy Community Historical Society, Inc. (VCHS) received grant monies not only to mount and exhibit many of the early twentieth-century photographs shown in this book and on display in the Vardy Church Museum but to publish the first edition. I especially wish to thank Dr. Clinton McCurdy Lipsey, last traveling minister at the Vardy Presbyterian Church, who had the foresight to protect the old glass lantern slides from which many of these photographs were transformed.

Thank you to the humanities scholars who were involved in teaching me about oral histories: Dr. Jean Haskell and Dr. Tess Lloyd, East Tennessee State University, as well as Katie M. Doman, doctoral candidate at the University of Tennessee, and Theresa Burchett, Appalachian State University graduate student, who interviewed many of those whose oral histories tell our story. I called a number of those interviewees many times for clarification on various points. Among those are my sister Margaret Williams Nevels and my brother Dan Williams. Several times during and since the first publication, Ruth Jenkins Muhlbauer, one of my dad's students at Vardy, has been able to help me understand the Vardy Community as she was growing up.

Other relatives who have been equally as important are Boyd Ward Collins, Cleland Collins, Oakey H. Collins, Thomas Collins, Claribel Miser Horton, and Billie Mullins Horton. Several of my dad's students from Vardy have been helpful, including W. C. Collins, Mae Williams Sexton, Charles Sizemore, R. C. Mullins, Lloyd Williams, and Troy L. Williams. Many of those mentioned are my friends from Vardy and are active participants in the Vardy Community Historical Society, Inc. I have laughed with Vardy classmates Geraldine (Tootsie Hatfield) Bell and Robert Moore at old memories while doing these oral histories. Often they reminded me of paddlings my parents gave me for not obeying their rules at school. (Needless to say, my parents believed in the old philosophy: "If one misbehaves in school, she also gets a paddling at home.")

I am amazed at the repetition of oral histories that were done by Katie Doman and me. Among those that I did not personally call or tape are Eula Mullins Collins, Audrey Mullins Franz, Hazel Goins Gibson, and Leonard Gibson. I did accompany Katie on several other interviews. Among those are Johnnie Gibson Rhea and Mossie Kate Overton. All of the oral histories done by Doman are archived at East Tennessee State University. As of this date, Theresa Burchett's and my oral histories have not been archived but are stored with VCHS.

Other VCHS board members who were not available to participate in the oral histories have given me additional information, stories, and pictures. Among them are Macie Mullins, Rose Trent, Jack Mullins, Sue Sizemore, and Betty Knight.

Willa Mae Gibson Mullins Moore has shared family pictures as well as photographs given to her by Louise Avery, the last Presbyterian missionary at Vardy. Louise has answered questions about her teaching at Vardy both by telephone and letter. I have received last-minute information from her as I write.

Reverend David F. Swartz, Presbyterian seminary intern at Vardy during 1945–1947 and a lifelong friend, contributed countless hours in researching and preparing informational manuscripts for this writing. I am especially grateful to him for his encouragement in seeing that these stories are printed.

I am indebted to my former student Sarah Kay for transcribing the oral history tapes, and to Jefferson County High School English teacher friends Thelma Gann for editing my work and Jodi Niceley for her computer skills.

Those whose work continue to inspire me are Brent Kennedy for his deep commitment to discovering truths about our origins and promoting our

Melungeon heritage as a matter of pride; Katherine VandeBrake for her exploration of the Melungeon characters and myths in literature; Jack Goins, author of *Melungeons and Other Pioneer Families*, and my sister-in-law Chris Williams for their genealogical research of my family; Jesse Stuart for his encouraging words written in 1966; Jean Patterson Bible for supporting me in my 1981 Children's Museum presentation and writing a truthful story about my community in her book *Melungeons Yesterday and Today*; John Rice Irwin for his preservation of our Appalachian ways; Jim Callahan for his telling of his family's stories in *Lest We Forget: The Melungeon Colony of Newman's Ridge*; Mattie Ruth Johnson for telling about her life on Newman's Ridge; and to Melungeon Heritage Association presidents Connie Clark and Wayne Winkler for including VCHS members and me as presenters of our stories at the MHA Unions.

Last but not least, I wish to thank the Presbyterians for long ago sending into our lives Miss Rankin and Mr. and Mrs. Leonard. Their records of our lives in school and church have been utilized in the writing of this book. Also I wish to thank Mattie Mae Grohse for giving me countless records which her father-in-law William P. "Bill" Grohse and his brother-in-law Reverend Arthur H. Taylor kept about my ancestral families. Most importantly I thank God for answering my prayers concerning this writing and guiding me into drawers, files, and stacks where I had stored Vardy memorabilia and print material.

Purposely I have steered away from the research of anthropologists and sociologists who have hashed and rehashed the mysterious origins of the Melungeons. While there are hundreds of books worth reading that explore these theories, they do little to promote our oral tradition. Even though a majority of the residents of Vardy during the 1920s, 1930s, 1940s, and 1950s presently claim Melungeon ancestry, it would be incorrect to assume that all of those quoted or pictured in this book are Melungeon.

Introduction

The experience of having been born into the Melungeon community of Vardy in Hancock County, Tennessee, as a descendant of Vardemon Collins has provided me with a lifelong quest to dispel the stereotypes associated with my family and friends. It is not easy to "get over" the many derogatory remarks made by Will Allen Dromgoole about my ancestors who were nothing but kind to her. Generation after generation, we were born carrying that "chip on our shoulder," smarting from remarks made about us by those wishing to study our roots and solve that mystery of our origins.

When did this quest begin for me? Was it coded into my genetic makeup even before I was born? I'm really not sure when I knew with certainty that I was Melungeon. The whispers among adults when I was growing up only made me curious. "Don't let them take your picture," my mother warned when photographers came to the Vardy Community Center to document our existence. Why did we need to be ashamed of who we were? Our Presbyterian theology had taught us that God hath made from one blood all nations. Despite our being economically deprived, we didn't believe we were any different than those who came to stare. How dare them to think so! We learned to stare back harder and longer.

Having heard *Melungeon* spoken in hushed terms and seeing first hand my mother's anger over the *Saturday Evening Post* article "Sons of the Legend" by W. I. Worden, I wanted to learn more about my maternal family and the stories associated with them.

Contributing to this desire was Jesse Stuart, my father's roommate at Lincoln Memorial University, who in 1966 responded to my letter concerning his novel *Daughter of the Legend.* "You have good years and writing years ahead of you. You have hundreds of Melungeon stories to write. They are all around you and don't be too self-conscious to write them." Stuart's letter encouraged me to find these stories which were all around me.

My parents met at Lincoln Memorial University (LMU). Their marriage resulted in six children. My older brother Dan also went to LMU. Out of that experience another connection was made by his friendship with John Rice Irwin, founder of the Museum of Appalachia and my superintendent while I was teaching in Anderson County, Tennessee. Irwin's work inspired me to discuss my Melungeon roots.

During the early 1980s, I spoke out against stereotyping the Melungeons at the Children's Museum in Oak Ridge, Tennessee, as a result of remarks made by an earlier speaker. Because of my insistence that I, a

Melungeon, have equal time, the museum director Selma Shapiro invited me to make a presentation. In a telephone conversation prior to the event, I asked Jean Patterson Bible, author of *Melungeons Yesterday and Today*, permission to quote her. Bible came to the presentation and was available to support my comments. In correspondence with Boyd Ward Collins dated August 18, 1981, I learned that "Bible 'was much taken with you [me].' . . . She mentioned the Appalachian experience—that neither you nor she had been invited and it had irritated her, too. She seems to have great faith that you will set the record straight."

To prepare my presentation, my parents provided me manuscripts, letters, and records from their personal files. My mother even gave me the October 17, 1947, issue of *The Saturday Evening Post* that she had been hiding for more than thirty years! Their cooperation in the preparation of my presentation has been priceless.

After the presentation at the Children's Museum, I received several letters from those who praised my remarks as being an honest representation of our lives without sensationalism. Mary Lou Duncan, a friend's mother, wrote, "I just felt compelled to write and tell you that your article on the Melungeon people was something that made me stand up and yell, 'Bravo! Tell 'em, gal. . . . Maybe some day we can be heard and believed on the subject of things that are right and things that are wrong."

In 1986, Jim Callahan, author of *Lest We Forget: The Melungeon Colony of Newman's Ridge*, asked my mother for help in obtaining information about his family. Mother referred him to me since she had already given me most of the family photographs and records from the church and school which had been in her and my father's possession. Callahan sought many others to aid him in his search as well. He wrote on December 6, 1986, "Ann and I enjoyed our first visit with the two of you and appreciated the generosity of your sharing of the old pictures." Callahan, too, wanted to tell the stories of his family.

It has taken many years for the Melungeons finally to find our voices. For many of us it has come through Brent Kennedy's successful efforts. Even though we were accumulating records, photographs, and family histories, we lacked the expertise to bring our stories to the forefront as he has done. Out of the corners of obscurity, we are coming into the limelight. As authors and others are discovering, Jesse Stuart had indeed been right. There are hundreds of Melungeon stories just waiting for a window to the present.

Chapter 1

Vardy's Location and Settlers

Vardy Valley is nestled between Powell Mountain
and Newman's Ridge on Blackwater Creek
in Hancock County, Tennessee, and Lee County, Virginia.

According to the oral tradition of Vardy Community families, who trace their ancestors to the early settlers of the late 1700s, the land on which they settled was obtained from several land grants. Trading, buying, and selling land grants among these early settlers were quite common. These land grants were obtained by men who served in the Revolutionary War as well as the War of 1812.

Direct descendants of Vardemon Collins and Margaret "Peggy" Gibson, the children of Drew and Alyce Horton Williams—my brothers, sisters, and I—own part of the original property which was granted to Vardemon Collins. John Wolf, who had received a land grant from North Carolina, assigned most of the acreage to Vardemon Collins in 1816. Other acres were obtained from James Johnson in 1825.[1] The acres from Bob Moore and Amanda Collins Moore were purchased by Drew Williams and his wife Alyce. As a result, the Williams family often referred to this section of the farm as the Bob Moore hill. Amanda Collins was a descen-

---

[1]Jack H. Goins, *Melungeons and Other Pioneer Families* (Rogersville TN: Jack Harold Goins, 2000) 55.

dant of Vardemon Collins, from whom, it is speculated, she inherited the property.

It had long been the dream of my mother Alyce Horton Williams, daughter of Adelaide Collins Horton and Daniel Boone Horton, to own what had once been the farm of her maternal grandfather Batey Collins,[2] proprietor of the Vardy Springs Hotel, which sat on the banks of Blackwater Creek near the Sulfur Springs. (Later Batey and his wife Cynthia abandoned the hotel for a log cabin often referred to as the Collins Boarding House.) Batey's grandfather was Vardemon Collins, from whom he had inherited much of the original Vardemon Collins farm. Batey, in turn, gave portions of his land to his daughters and son. These children were Noah Collins, the Vardy postmaster and school teacher who married Alice Loven Bales; Frankie Collins, who married Harrison Collins; Nancy Collins, who married Logan Miser; and Adelaide, my grandmother and the wife of my grandfather Daniel Boone Horton.

A more inclusive landscape of the Vardy Community
Center which shows the C. F. Leonard Manse
on the lower right, barely visible above the barn.

Vardy Community existed before Hancock County was created in 1844. After 1796, it was part of Hawkins County, Tennessee, which was actually in Spencer County in the State of Franklin. Historians indicate that this community saw a lot of changes in its governing boundaries. In 1785,

---

[2]Batey's name is spelled in a variety of publications and records as *Baty*, *Beatty*, *Beatie*, and *Beatey*. All of these were pronounced as "Batey" and refer to the same individual.

it was not only a part of the Washington District of North Carolina but also had been claimed by both Virginia and Kentucky.

The location of the Vardy Community, named for my ancestor Vardemon Collins, extended the entire length of the Vardy Valley. The valley lies on Blackwater Creek between Newman's Ridge and Powell Mountain. It begins in Hancock County, Tennessee, straddles the Lee County, Virginia, line, and extends a short distance into Blackwater, Virginia.

Looking up Vardy Valley on the original homestead of Vardemon Collins is the farm now owned by my sister, my brothers, and me.

Charles Sizemore, a board member of the Vardy Community Historical Society (VCHS), described Vardy as being "from the Sneedville Road to just a little past the Virginia line, east and west and north to the top of Powell Mountain, then south to the top of Newman's Ridge."[3]

According to W. P. Grohse, Jr., "Geographically, our valley starts at Blackwater, Virginia, and ends at Howard's Quarters in Claiborne County. Vardy is the section east of the Mulberry Gap-Sneedville Road. The same people who settled Vardy settled in Blackwater, Lee County, Virginia, and Howard's Quarters. The Blackwater Valley Road in Virginia is called the Vardy Valley Road on the Tennessee side."[4]

There seems to be little doubt of Vardy Community's location. One of the older members of the VCHS, Cleland Collins described it: "The

---

[3]Charles Sizemore, Vardy Oral Histories, interviewed by Katie Dorman, Vardy Church, Sneedville TN, February 2000.

[4]W. P. Grohse, Jr., "A Brief History of Vardy Community, Hancock County," manuscript to Alyce and Drew Williams, Williams Family Collection.

boundaries of Vardy, as I understood them, on the north would have been the top of Powell Mountain; on the south, the top of Newman's Ridge; the east, the Tennessee-Virginia state line; and on the west, the Mulberry-Sneedville Road."[5]

Many of the early settlers built log homes that were also used by later generations.

This family of four children was considered small since many Vardy residents had more children who helped make their living on farms.

Land grants were located not just on the narrow valley floor but extended often from the top of Newman's Ridge, across the breadth of the valley, and to the top of Powell Mountain.

Tennessee historians relate that at one time France, Spain, and Great Britain all claimed the region since there was quite a bit of competition among them to develop ties with the Indians, primarily for the flourishing fur trade. After the French and Indian War in 1754, the British became the dominant force. After the Treaty of Paris, the British then claimed all lands east of the Mississippi. Few can deny that among these fur traders and early travelers were those who fathered a great number of children with the Indians. However, permanent settlers began to come into the Vardy Valley from Virginia and North Carolina about that time.

Grohse adds that "Dr. Thomas Walker of Virginia and his exploring party are believed to have passed through or nearby the Vardy Valley as

---

[5]Cleland Collins, Vardy Oral Histories, interviewed by Sally Collins and DruAnna Overbay, Morristown TN, 25 April 1999.

early as 1748. In the fall of 1762, Elisha Wallen and his company of hunters hunted in the Blackwater Creek area [Vardy]."[6]

When our early settlers came into the valley, the lower end on the southeast of the Vardemon Collins farm was settled predominately by the Bales, Bell, Delph, Minor, Mullins, Parks, and Sizemore families. The center of the valley was settled by the Anderson, Collins, Misers, and Williams families. The upper northwest end was customarily Bunch, Collins, and Gibson families.

The Gibson families were among the early settlers of Vardy and Newman's Ridge. In the 1930s, Gilbert Gibson and his wife lived in the Mahala Mullins log cabin.

The Collins, Goins, Johnson, Mullins, and Stewart families were located on Newman's Ridge while the Davidson, Gibson, Moore, Sexton, and Williams families were mainly on the Powell Mountain side. Even today some of the descendants of these early settlers own some of the same farms that their ancestors first settled.

As a matter of fact, one of those interviewed speculated that the farms of families that she remembered as a child were inherited or bought from other family members whose older members had settled in that area. Mae Williams Sexton remembered family names of those living in the Vardy Community beginning on the east side of the valley as being

Allie Mullins, Lewis Alder, Harvey Gibson, Bertha Jenkins, Alp Delp, Ellen Trent, Dora Mullins, George Moore, Burkett Mullins, Carson Mullins, Tennessee Goins, Albert Mullins, Roy Collins,

[6]Grohse, "A Brief History of Vardy Community, Hancock County."

Howard Mullins, Calvin Mullins, Boyd Collins, Lizzie and Herbie Collins, Mother and Pop Grohse (Bill's parents from Germany), Bill Grohse, Nancy Miser, Drew Williams, Lloyd Sizemore, Ruthie Anderson and Eliza Goins, Ed Williams, Louella Williams, Harrison Collins, Wardell Collins, Andy Gibson, Minnie Gibson, Burghie and Leslie Collins, Sally Davidson, Lonnie Hatfield, Grover Hatfield, David Hatfield, Owen Harris, Neil Roberts, Daniel Roberts, Docia Mullins, and Hillary Gibson (both young Hillary and old Hillary).

On the Powell Mountain side lived Julia and William Gibson, Grant Moore, Charlie Moore, Alfred Mullins, Ike Mullins, Charles Carroll, Jenny Ritchie, Rosa and Nina Delp.

Making their homes on the Newman's Ridge side were Hughie Mullins, Anderson Bell, Asa Gibson, Coby and Hazel Gibson, Gilbert Gibson, Brownlow Mullins, Alfred Gibson, David Gibson, Henry Sweeney, Cora and Brownlow Goins, Paris Goins, Aunt Bertha and Lewis Collins, Lewis Johnson, Steve Gibson, Martin Collins, and Flora Alder.[7]

In Grohse's records,

The first settlers are believed to have been Navarrh Collins (also known as Vardiman Collings) and Shepherd Gibson. They probably thought they were still in Virginia and would be given the land they settled. Early land grants bear out this theory. Among the first settlers are the names of James Mullins, James Collins (Collings), Soloman Collins, Benjamin Collins (Collings), Vardiman Collins (Collings), Shepherd Gibson, Joseph Gibson, Benjamin Bunch, Thomas Miser (Mizer), George Miser (Mizer), Joseph Goins (Goings), James Moore, James Johnson, and many others. Practically every family in the valley during the 1940s was directly descended from these early pioneers.[8]

Most of the people interviewed for the oral history project did not think that their families were a particular race, but rather a mixture of settlers from different countries as well as Indian. Some claimed that the Indian

---

[7]Mae Williams Sexton, Vardy Oral Histories, interviewed by Troy Lee Williams, Laurel MD, 28 September 1999.

[8]Grohse, "A Brief History of Vardy Community."

ancestry was Cherokee while others claimed Saponi. The origins of these various groups of settlers have been a subject of debate for generations. It is hard to place these settlers as having arrived from one specific geographical location.

Until newly married couples became more prosperous and self-sufficient, they often lived in their parents' or grandparents' homes. Sukie Gibson (Suckie Gipson) balls a skein of homespun as her daughter takes care of the "young' uns."

"Vardy Collins's Cherokee ancestry is often noted by his descendants," wrote Katie Doman. "His family migrated from North Carolina to the Vardy valley in the 1700s. As interesting as they are, the ethnic origins of this community are certainly not its most important feature."[9]

An article entitled "How Vardy Yielded to the Gospel," published in 1916 and reprinted from *The Continent* reports, "For the Vardy Community is a tribal settlement of 150 souls descended from the Cherokee Indians, who less than 100 years ago called all mountain land their own."[10]

Early records indicate, "They are of pure English ancestry and have lived isolated from the rest of the country for more than two hundred years."[11]

---

[9]Katie Doman, manuscript to Vardy Community Historical Society, 20 June 2002.

[10]"How Vardy Yielded to the Gospel," *The Continent*, 1916.

[11]"Information Please," *The Church on the Hill*, Englewood Cliffs NJ, January 1943.

Like many of the settlers all over the eastern coast, people went to the area where land was cheaper or had not been claimed by a homesteader. Many followed Daniel Boone to the Cumberland Gap area. We are so close to Cumberland Gap that I think there is a definite connection. Our oral tradition tells us that we are part Indian, Portuguese, German, Scotch-Irish, and English on my mother's side.

The Transylvania Company, formed by a North Carolina judge to establish a colony in Kentucky, bought a large area of the land from the Cherokee in 1775. Daniel Boone worked for the company and opened the land to settlement. The famous Wilderness Trail is only four miles from the Vardy Community. As a matter of fact, the Vardy Valley up Blackwater Creek, across Mulberry Gap, down Mulberry to Alanthus, on to Ewing, Virginia, is a less treacherous route to Cumberland Gap, Kentucky, than crossing Powell Mountain to Jonesville, Virginia. Actually, the early settlers came into the valley at about the same time from North Carolina via Rogersville. "They had started west, but about four families stopped for reasons which now seem small (a child died here, a wagon broke down, etc.) and settled down."[12]

Many historians, as well as our family's genealogist, can trace my (third) great-grandfather Vardemon Collins to North Carolina; however, his nationality is in dispute. I recently had an e-mail from an individual in Australia whose last name is Vardemon. He is looking for a connection to Vardemon Collins as he claims that some of his ancestors migrated from England to America, but he cannot locate that family here. He contends that Vardemon is the surname of Vardemon Collins's mother. It will help solve the puzzle if indeed that connection can be proven, but at present I do not know even the name of Vardemon's mother. We do believe that Varde-mon's father is Henry Collins, who came from England. Other sources list Vardy's father as Samuel Collins of Botetourt County, Virginia. Jack H. Goins's book *Melungeons and Other Pioneer Families* has a detailed story in his chapter "Melungeons: The Head and Source" about Grandpa Vardemon.

After the first edition of *Windows on the Past* was published, Jack Goins e-mailed me that his research indicated that Vardy's mother was Letitia Vardemon (Vardeman). In our correspondence, he told me that he

---

[12]"Survey of the Vardy Presbyterian Church," Vardy Community Presbyterian Church Records, 1902.

had gotten three sources of information indicating this to be true—"one is court records, another is from a Vardiman researcher who wants to remain anonymous, and the Ramseys."

Virgie Horton rode a horse from Index, Kentucky, through the mountains to Vardy to locate her brother Daniel and sisters Lizzie and Fluie. Settling there around 1904, she later decided to return to Kentucky.

Jack Goins asks, "Where did you get that Vardy's dad was Navarrah? I thought this was a suggestion from Bill Grohse, which really came from a misspelling of Vardy by the census taker. Grohse wanted to put a Spanish name on him."

Much of the material which Bill Grohse had obtained early in his research came from Reverend Arthur Taylor, Bill's brother-in-law. Taylor knew that Bill would continue keeping the family's records that the Presbyterians had begun when they first came into the valley. Many of these facts were obtained from the oral histories they had begun.

Goins says, "This name Vardeman, believed to be Vardy's mother's name, may be true. John Vardeman was on the same tax list with Samuel Collins, believed to be the father of Vardy in Botetourt County, Virginia. It is also evident in family name patterns. John and Elizabeth Morgan Vardeman named their first daughter Elizabeth from her mother's name, named a second daughter Letitia, born in 1746, and named a son Morgan from Elizabeth's maiden name. Vardy Collins, born in 1764, named his oldest son Morgan and his oldest daughter Letita, which suggests that John and Elizabeth's daughter Letitia, born in 1746, may have been Vardy Collins's mother. Vardy was born in 1764.

"You have Henry in your book as Vardy's father and there was a Henry in Hawkins County, but he doesn't appear to be as old as Vardy, but at least

Henry is in a record, so he could be a son of old Samuel. Samuel Collins was older than Letitia Vardeman."[13]

Various members of the VCHS had a more interesting story of the origins of their forebears. Cleland Collins remembered his Aunt Docia Collins Miser's telling him, "Our folks came over with Sir Walter Raleigh, and when he returned to England, his trip back was delayed so that they had to move out of the fort at Roanoke and mixed with the Indians. Some of the families lived with the Indians. Later they migrated westward into North Carolina and eventually settled in the Clinch River Valley. When white settlers came along and found English-speaking people living and mixing with the Indians, they called us Melungeon and drove us further into the ridges and mountains."[14]

It is speculated that because the land on Newman's Ridge and the Vardy valley was not the most desirable for farming, the more recent settlers managed to push them onto the border of Virginia, Tennessee, and Kentucky.

"I'm a Melungeon," Oakey Collins declared. "My father was one-quarter Indian, and even in the early 1900s, my older brother had on his birth certificate that our dad was a man of color. Now, at that time, the Melungeon, which is a mixed race with the Indians, no doubt, was discriminated against. Tennessee had passed a law previously that a person of even one-sixth Indian wasn't allowed to own land, vote, or even go to school. So, I think, this had been in my father's mind at the time because all of my older sisters and cousins went to Asheville, North Carolina, to a Presbyterian boarding school. Then, later we all went to Ewing, Virginia."[15] Records indicate that Oakey's grandfather Howard Collins and other relatives were arrested for illegal voting.

Much of the discrimination against the Vardy residents was a result of the "infamous" Andrew Jackson, who had previously led many of them in the War of 1812. It was reported by historians that Jackson resented the Indians in the east for owning the best farmlands. As a result, he encouraged states to pass laws denying the Indians legal protection if the states seized their property. Not knowing whether to classify some of Jackson's former allies as white or Indian, the census takers during his administration

---

[13]Jack Goins, e-mail correspondence to DruAnna Overbay, 12 November 2003.
[14]Cleland Collins, Vardy Oral Histories.
[15]Oakey Hendrix Collins, Vardy Oral Histories, interviewed by Sally Collins and DruAnna Overbay, Morristown TN, 25 April 1999.

were instructed to list dark-skinned people as free men of color. Not being allowed to vote or go to public schools were but two of the results.

Aunt Mahala suffered from elephantiasis and, during the late years of her life, was unable to leave her home.

From the genealogical research of his wife Chris Williams, Daniel H. Williams related, "Mahala Collins Mullins's parents were Solomon D. Collins and Jincie Goins, who were early settlers in Vardy. Solomon received land grants in 1829 (Claiborne County), 1833, and 1845 (Hawkins County). Hancock County was Hawkins County in those days." He added, "The 1830 census lists Solomon Collins as a free man of color. It is rumored that he was a full-blooded Cherokee Indian."[16]

"Mother always told us that we were Irish and Indian. That is the only thing that she ever told us," R. C. Mullins replied when asked about his ancestors' origin. "If anybody ever asked us what nationality we were, we'd say we were Irish and Indian mixed. . . . Mother used to tell us, or tell me, to wear long sleeves and a hat so I wouldn't get dark. . . . We worked out in the summertime and we'd get dark . . . we'd tan real easy and get really dark. . . . But, they didn't like it when we'd get so dark. I guess they didn't want the Indian part coming out, or . . . whatever it was."[17]

---

[16]Daniel H. Williams, Vardy Oral Histories, interviewed by DruAnna Overbay, Knoxville TN, 15 June 2002.

[17]R. C. Mullins, Vardy Oral Histories, interviewed by DruAnna Overbay, Talbott TN, 15 June 2002.

There is too much dispute and disagreement about the origin of our various families to go into much detail about it. I believe, at this point, there is little to be gained by detailing this information. However, I do think it important for us to continue our genealogical search. Ruth Jenkins Muhlbauer reminded me that "A lot of other people are studying our origin right now. There's only a very few true Melungeons left . . . very few. I'm not a full-blooded Melungeon. . . . Of course, my great-great-grandmother Mahala Mullins was the most famous one. When I was growing up, we didn't talk about who we were too much. It was just something we knew—a knowledge that was just below the surface. We always thought we were a mixture of Indian and English, but nobody wants to believe our stories."[18]

Even though a majority of the residents of Vardy during the 1920s, 1930s, 1940s, and 1950s presently claim Melungeon ancestry, it would be incorrect to assume that all of those who are quoted or pictured in this book have that distinction.

In October 1947, I became aware that I, too, am a Melungeon. Because I went to the Vardy Community Elementary School, where both my parents were teaching, I was permitted to go down the hill to retrieve the mail from our home mailbox during recess. Usually my sisters Margaret and Charlotte went after the mail, but they were busy planning an assembly program and the task fell to me. I always looked forward to being the first in the family to look at the magazines. On that particular day the *Saturday Evening Post* arrived. The article "Sons of the Legend" caught my eye because of my recognizing pictures of our neighbors Asa Gibson, Laura Mullins, and others. Sitting on the school steps, I began thumbing through the magazine, becoming more and more excited. When I yelled to other students to come and look at the magazine, my mother rushed out of the classroom and snatched the magazine from my hands.

That night my mother's angry words to my dad and my maternal grandfather awakened me. She was very upset and began screaming, "Why can't they leave us alone? I wish I never had to hear that word [Melungeon] again!"

Of course, the *us* did not include my dad and her dad, for only my mother denied the Melungeon heritage that our genealogy studies have proven. Despite the fact that I was only five, from that day on I have known

---

[18]Ruth Jenkins Muhlbauer, telephone interviews by DruAnna Overbay, July 2002.

that I, too, am a Melungeon. That undercurrent of being a Melungeon was there—unspoken and yet known.

Sometimes my siblings and I would talk about our ancestry, and our mother would overhear and tell us not to speak of being Melungeon in her presence. My dad would readily discuss it with us. As we became older, she became more accepting of our heritage and even gave me the magazine that she had for years kept hidden from my eyes. She knew that I would eventually talk about my heritage and began giving me her old family pictures and other clippings from various articles. She, too, began writing notes in composition notebooks, telling me about her life as a child. Perhaps she really wanted me to be the spokesperson from our family to discuss our heritage.

Virginia and Kentucky relatives always came home to Vardy where Fourth of July celebrations were held on the picnic grounds of the Vardy Springs Hotel prior to the 1920s.

+ + + + +

Reunion at Vardy Springs

"Papa Horton tore down the
Vardy Springs Hotel
Taking the timbers to Ewing, Virginia,
To build a new home for his wife,
Ten years his senior.

"Adelaide Collins
Was Grandma's maiden name.
She had gotten her share of land
From Great-Grandpa Batey,
Who had built the Vardy Springs Hotel,
Hoping to harness the healing powers
Of the nearby sulfur waters.

"Born in 1845, Batey,
The son of Alfred Collins and Elizabeth Mullins,
Wore the Union uniform
(Company E, Eighth Tennessee Calvary)
During the Civil War.

"Coming home from the battlefields,
He set out to make his fortune
On the plot of land given to him
By his father after marrying
'Cousin Sentia' Cynthia Collins.

"Her father Simeon, Frankie Bunch's man,
Was Great-great Grandpa Alfred's brother . . .
So the Vardy Springs Hotel
Had been a family venture
Honoring Great-great-great Grandpa.

"Vardy Collins
Born over in Wilkes County, North Carolina . . .
1764 . . .
Yes, Papa Horton tore down the
Vardy Springs Hotel."

I tell my sons and grandchildren,
Just as my Mom told me
As we walk hand-in-hand
On the Blackwater Creek bank
At the foot of Newman's Ridge.
"And you wonder why
I love this land?"
I ask while pointing to the
Cornerstone of the Vardy Springs Hotel.

Chapter 2

The Presbyterians Arrive

The Vardy Community Center was one result of the 1890s Presbyterian mission school movement. In East Tennessee alone, five mission schools operated in the Holston Presbytery: Grassy Cove (near Crossville), Jeroldstown (near Kingsport), Kismet (unknown location), Rock Creek (Erwin), and Vardy. The Vardy mission school served children within the eight-mile stretch of the Vardy Valley in Tennessee, which is also known as Blackwater Valley in Virginia.

*Sulfur Springs Baptist Church was the site of the first meeting
in Vardy held by Dr. Christopher Humble and gospel singer
Dr. Snodgrass, both of whom were Presbyterian.*

According to the Vardy Community Presbyterian Church records, Miss Annie B. Miller and Maggie Axtell were appointed as missionaries under the Presbyterian Women's Board to serve the Vardy Community. Prior to their arrival, Reverend C. Humble and Reverend H. P. Cory served as circuit ministers in the area. "This church is largely due to the results of Miss Annie B. Miller and Maggie Axtell under the Women's Board," wrote Noah Collins, the church clerk, and Reverend J. H. Wallin, moderator, in the sessions record under the heading, "Organized by Rev. C. Humble and Rev. H. P. Cory, recorded in Vardy, Tennessee, July 4, 1902."[1]

---

[1]Noah Collins, Vardy Community Church Records, Vardy TN, 1902–1910.

In a letter, Margaret McCall explained that she was living and teaching in Topeka, Kansas, when she learned of the Presbyterian plan to establish a mission school at Vardy. She and Annie B. Miller of Rogersville became boarders at the home of Batey and Cynthia Collins.[2]

In a view traveling east and entering the historical district is seen the original steeple, which was shortened during the 1960s because of a lack of maintenance funds.

As one traveled two miles west from the Lee County, Virginia line, one saw the Vardy Community Presbyterian Church, the C. F. Leonard manse, the hothouse, and the clinic.

Church Development

A descendant of the Bales family who migrated to Indiana during the 1920s, Jim Callahan has written extensively about the Vardy Community.

According to history, two Presbyterian missionaries randomly passed through the area in 1892. . . . At an unknown time during that year, Dr. Christopher Humble and gospel singer Dr. Snodgrass dropped in on a church meeting in the old Sulphur Springs Baptist Church. The introductory meeting seemed amiable, and a second

---

[2]W. P. Grohse, Jr., Vardy Historian's personal notes (1931–1977), Mattie Mae Grohse Collection.

meeting was held at the Collins Boarding House. The missionaries spoke of their desire to educate the colonists and win souls to Christ. . . .

The first permanent missionary leaders to be stationed in Vardy were chosen by the Presbyterian Mission Board of New York. They were two young single women, Miss Margaret McCall, a Washburn College graduate of Topeka, Kansas, and Miss Annie Breem Miller of Rogersville, Tennessee.[3]

These facts are also recorded in the *Morristown Citizen Tribune* articles ("Echoes from Vardy") written by William P. Grohse, Jr., father of the late Willie O. Grohse, who was among the first VCHS board members. Willie Grohse told VCHS board members during one of their 1998 board meetings, "My dad kept all kinds of records of the people in the valley, our relatives, who they married, who their children were, where they moved. He was continuously writing about Vardy. He left filing cabinets full of information and pictures of Vardy."[4] Those doing research about their families and the region have utilized much of this William P. Grohse material.

Church records further reflect that Miss S. E. MacBride was received into the church by letter on January 12, 1902. It is not clear from the church records how long she stayed. It is assumed she replaced missionary Annie B. Miller, who was dismissed on June 8, 1902. Although, according to Callahan, Miss Margaret McCall came to Vardy, there is no evidence of this name in the church records. Perhaps Maggie Axtell married a McCall.

Beside the name of Maggie Axtell on the enrollment of church members in 1899 is written simply "Dismissed." Her name is not on the membership roll of 1902. Additionally, Julie Miller, Annie's sister, was also a missionary who boarded at the Vardy Springs Hotel, which operated from 1835 until the death of Batey Collins in 1914.

Even though Miss Sarah E. MacBride was dismissed from her membership by letter on March 8, 1903, she may have changed missions earlier. Following MacBride, the new missionary to join the church was Mary May Thompson. Church clerk Noah Collins recorded that "The session met on October 9, 1904, at the residence of Beattie (Batey) Collins. After being

---

[3]Jim Callahan, *Lest We Forget: The Melungeon Colony of Newman's Ridge* (Johnson City TN: OverMountain Press, 2000).

[4]Willie Grohse, comments during Vardy Community Historical Society board meeting, April 1998.

constituted by prayers, the following persons were received in full fellowship. Miss Mary May Thompson by letter from Mt. Bethel Church in Tusculum, Tenn."[5] One can only surmise that Miss Thompson replaced Miss MacBride.

Research yields conflicting reports concerning these early missionaries. An article in *The Continent* states: "It is just fifteen years now that the Presbyterian Women's Board in New York heard about Vardy and asked two young women to go there and start a school. Miss Gray and Miss Axtell went. . . . But what fifteen years have accomplished under the ministry of these fearless women and their successors, Miss Rankin and Miss Harris."[6]

Perhaps this is a Sunday school class of Miss Harris's,
a missionary who served with Miss Rankin during the early 1910s.
Two first cousins in identical dresses are pictured on the front row:
Batey Collins's granddaughters Mae Miser, daughter of Nancy
and Logan Miser, and Mossey Horton, daughter of Adelaide
and Daniel B. Horton. The other Vardy girls are unknown.

On March 10, 1905, Miss M. P. Gray moved her letter to the Vardy Church from a Presbyterian church in New York (a specific church is not mentioned). No further mention of missionaries is made until the arrival of Miss Mary J. Rankin.

Even though the church records do not give the name of Miss White, Ruth Jenkins Muhlbauer suggests that she was a missionary teacher about whom her mother had spoken:

---

[5]Noah Collins.
[6]"How Vardy Yielded to the Gospel," *The Continent* (1916).

It seems that Miss White went walking in Powell Mountain and became lost. As it was approaching dark, she was frightened of wild animals finding her. For her safety, she climbed a tree for the night. Afraid that she would go to sleep and fall from the tree, Miss White wound her long hair around a limb so if she began to doze, the pulling of her hair would awaken her.

The next morning when it was discovered that she had not returned from her walk, my father [Tom Jenkins] and Logan Miser went in search of her. They found her in the tree with her hair so tangled that it had to be cut to free her.[7]

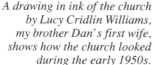

A drawing in ink of the church by Lucy Cridlin Williams, my brother Dan's first wife, shows how the church looked during the early 1950s.

+ + + + +

Vardy Presbyterian Church

"This church built in 1897,"
Reads the time-worn sign
I turn the key of the rusted lock
As the hinges squeak of the opened door
Marbled now

---

[7]Ruth Jenkins Muhlbauer, telephone interview by DruAnna Overbay, 24 December 2004.

Soaked by the rain
Dried by the sun

This church filling my sight
With broken pews,
Shattered window panes,
Scattered debris,
Fallen peeling paint
Marbled now
    Soaked by the rain
    Dried by the sun

Picking up dusty hymnals
Opening the covers
Silver fish fleeing
In the face of danger
Bookplate dedications, "In Memory of . . . "
Names floating through my consciousness
Marbled now
    Soaked by the rain
    Dried by the sun

"This church . . .
The last time I was in it,"
My voice quavered for calmness,
"Was for Papa Horton's funeral."
I remember that day
This church so full of
Life in the face of death
Marbled now
    Soaked by the rain
    Dried by the sun.

(Written after my husband and I purchased the church house in 1996.)

Chapter 3

Church Construction

In a copy of a manuscript that he was writing, which he sent to Alyce and Drew Williams, W. P. Grohse, Vardy Presbyterian Church elder, stated that "In 1898 the present Presbyterian Church was started. . . . The church was built on contract by Marion Osborne, Miles Watson, and others." Osborne is believed to have been from Blackwater, Virginia. The building was built on property donated by Batey and Cynthia Collins. Several people in the community gave their lumber and labor to erect the building.[1]

Walking down Vardy Road, a group of churchgoers passes the home and farm of Rutha Anderson.

David Swartz noted that "The church was important, an important part. It was the center of the community, really, as was the school. The building itself consisted primarily of two parts: the sanctuary area with the pews and an area in the front for lectern and pulpit, an organ, nice windows, and a communion table on which were flowers, sometimes, and, then, on the right there was this area for a church library and for a classroom for small children. There were Sunday School classes there . . . several ages in one class . . . nice pews and fine windows with a lot of light. There was a place to put hats, too, on pegs in the back."[2]

---

[1]W. P. Grohse, "A Brief History of Vardy Community, Hancock County, Tennessee," manuscript from the Williams family collection.

[2]David F. Swartz, Vardy Oral Histories, interviewed by DruAnna Overbay, Boone NC, 5 June 1999.

To enter the church, one climbed up a set of thirteen steps, onto a four-foot-square porch. For a youngster, the steps were literally quite a climb. A round metal banister went up the stairs and around the porch.

Robert Moore told me: "My father, Grant Moore, waited for my brothers, sisters, and me to come out of church every Sunday on that porch. He would lean against those banisters talking to the other men after church until we came out of Sunday school."[3]

The Vardy Church congregation in 1925. Standing on the porch are Herbie Collins, Daniel B. Horton, Preacher Leonard, and others who are unidentified. Below the porch, on the left, is Mary J. Rankin.

There were wide double-entry doors, a large entryway where the church bell rope hung from the twelve-foot ceiling. On the left of the entrance was a door into the church library.

Around the entryway were a number of pegs on which the members hung their coats or hats. Troy Williams remembered seeing his father hang his hat on one of these pegs before he took up his ushering duties at the church each Sunday morning. Ed Williams was a very active member of the church along with his entire family—brother, sisters, wife, and children.

Before entering the sanctuary, one walked through swinging double doors. On the left were three tall windows, topped with a triangular apex. Two of these windows were on the right of the sanctuary. The sanctuary had a cathedral ceiling, a wide aisle on the left, several rows of pews on the

---

[3]Robert Moore, Vardy Oral Histories, interviewed by DruAnna Overbay, Talbott TN, 13 July 2002.

right, and an altar in the front composed of an upper and lower stage. In the upper stage was one window on both the right and left side.

The stage provided VCHS members fond memories of being in various church and school programs. Moore recalled that

> Laurie Mullins made my Easter play costume. It had bunny ears and a cottontail. For my part, I carried a basket and skipped down the aisle singing, "Going off to Goose-Land." I don't remember if we gave the play in church or at school, but Alyce Williams was my teacher. I got to be one of three wise men on more than one occasion for the Christmas plays.
>
> Anderson Bell and Herbie Collins would meet us at the door because one or the other rang the church bell as we were coming up the steps to Sunday school.[4]

In addition to signaling church meetings and community gatherings, the bell was also used to notify the community of deaths and funerals. Ruth Jenkins Muhlbauer wrote, "I will never forget Adelaide Collins Horton's funeral because I was one of the flower girls. Miss Rankin had each of her Sunday School girls carry a large bouquet of flowers into the church for the funeral and later on to the Vardy Community Cemetery across from Tennessee Goins's house for her burial. While the coffin was carried out of the church, we girls stood on either side of each of the church steps. The bell rang to signify the end of the funeral service, too."[5]

The church bell was housed in the steeple. The original steeple was much taller than the one which was rebuilt in 2000. "When the final touches were being added to the steeple, one of the natives sang a rendition of 'The Pretty Mohee.' "[6]

Early Ministers

The first permanent minister mentioned in the records is Rev. Wallin. On January 12, 1902, church clerk Noah Collins wrote that "Reverend J. H. Wallin, S.S. Missionary, began a protracted service at the Vardy Presbyte-

---

[4]Robert Moore, Vardy Oral Histories.

[5]Ruth Jenkins Muhlbauer, personal letter to DruAnna Overbay, February 1999.

[6]W. P. Grohse, Jr., Vardy Historian's personal notes (1931–1977), Mattie Mae Grohse Collection.

rian Church."[7] Whether Reverend Wallin lived in the valley is not recorded. Several Presbyterian ministers served the church during those early years. Those mentioned in the church records and the dates of their having been at Vardy for sessions are recorded.

On September 6, 1916, Arthur H. Taylor preached during the service. Reverend Taylor married Grace Miser during the summer of 1919 in Sneedville. By 1922, Taylor had become minister of Ebenezer Presbyterian Church in Rockwood, Illinois. Grace sent this photograph to her Aunt Adelaide Horton, my grandmother.

In addition to Reverend Wallin (mentioned on January 12, 1902; February 2, 1902; October 22, 1911; and September 6, 1916), the following are named: Reverend Josh Miller (on October 15, 1905; December 10, 1906; and February 6, 1907); Reverend Sylvester J. Amentrout (on July 12, 1908); Reverend W. B. Stone (on December 6, 1909; and February 12, 1910); Reverend Calvin A. Duncan (on January 29, 1911); Dr. George Mack (on July 1, 1917); and Reverend H. W. White (on August 6, 1917).

Many area Presbyterian ministers gave of their services, traveling from Washington Academy in Jonesboro, Tusculum College in Tusculum, Warren Wilson College in Swannanoa, North Carolina, and churches in Bristol, Greeneville, Kingsport, Johnson City, and Morristown. Had they been a part of a circuit of retired ministers helping the Presbyterian Board of National Missions until a resident minister was located? The VCHS members who were interviewed did not know. However, they did remember

---

[7]Noah Collins, Vardy Community Presbyterian Church Records, Vardy TN, 1902–1910.

visitors during their years at the Vardy Community School. Only the church records are available to tell the history.

Perhaps no minister lived in the Vardy Community until Reverend Chester F. Leonard arrived. He is first mentioned in the church records (on August 10, 1918). The impact of his ministry on this community, as well as the mission work of Mary J. Rankin, is well known and the subject of many of the oral histories recorded by VCHS.

Vardy Community men who were leaders in the church included, in the front row, Vardy Vincent Collins, young Vardy Collins, Clay Miser, Uncle Noah Collins, Frank Miser, James (Jeemes) Henry Goins, and Logan Miser. On the back row are Leham Collins (young boy), Bud "Rand" Collins, Reverend Chester F. Leonard, and William (Kell) Collins.

Early Members

A list of early church members, recorded in the church records as they joined the church in 1902, is as follows: Marnie Mullins, Rubin Mullins, Birtha Collins (Jenkins), Dora Collins, Girtie Collins (Mullins), Manda Gipson, Dora Mullins, Birdey Collins, Pagie Collins, Mrs. Thomas Moore, Mary Moore, Alonzo Mullins, Thomas Moore, Margarett Moore, Zelpha Mullins, Sarah E. MacBride, Howard Mullins, Elizabeth Gipson, Birthey Collins, Matt Collins, Hettie Jones, Bum Collins, Bettie (Elizabeth) Collins, Hattie Collins, Jessie Collins and Dollie Gipson. (While spelling of members' names may vary, these spellings are as they appear in church records.)

The church records continue the list for 1903: Charley Collins (Melvin Collins's son), Tish Mullins, Mollie Swinney, George Swinney, Hattie Ann Gowins, James H. Gowins, Mattie Gowins, W. M. Davidson, James Gipson, Lizzie Gipson.

In 1904 Larie Mullins, Boyed Steward, Mrs. Cora Steward, Polly Jane Mullins, Dazie Mullins, Alexander Gipson, Cary Gipson, Mrs. Annie Williams, Mrs. Ruth Anderson, Wesley Mullins, Suckey Gipson, Mrs. Vestia Williams, Miss M. P. Gray, Recie Goins, and Miss Mary May Thompson are listed.

An unidentified boy and Oppie Miser stand beside my grandfather Daniel B. Horton, whose Sunday school class during the early 1910s included (on the back row) Curtis Miser, Jasper Mullins, Coby Gibson, Gilbert Gibson, Walter Miser, Crodell Collins, Ernest Miser, Merlin Collins, Ollie Collins, Tillman Collins, and Connor Bales. Many of these young men migrated to Indiana when my grandfather moved there in the 1930s.

Mrs. Sallie Davidson joined the church in 1905 along with Mrs. Elizabeth Miser, Mollie Collins, and George Miser. Followed by Mrs. Lewis Collins in 1906 are the names of Meade Anderson, Miss Lizzie Horton (who later married Joe Stewart), and Mrs. Munleys (Fluie Horton) Collins in 1907.

Full membership of the revised rolls of Vardy Church on July 12, 1908, state that the following were members in good standing: Larkin Mullins, Caney Collins, Kit Collins, Franka Collins, Shelby Williams, Thomas Anderson, Beaty (Batey) Collins, Noah Collins, Alice Collins, Monless (Munley's, Munless) Collins, Docia Miser, Jane Collins, Hattie Mullins Bales, Mary Ann Miser, Clay Miser, Nancy Miser, Harrison Gibson, Bertha Collins, Dora Collins (Mullins), Girtie Collins (Mrs. Fred M. Mullins), Manda Gibson, Elizabeth Gibson, Hattie Ann Gowins, Mattie Gowins,

James H. Gibson, James Gibson, Mrs. Dollie Gibson, Polly Jane Mullins, Cary Gibson (Collins), Mrs. Ruth Anderson, Suckey Gibson, Mrs. Dalton (Vestia) Collins Mrs. Dollie Davidson, Meade Anderson, Mrs. Joe (Lizzie) Stewart, Mrs. Monless (Fluie) Collins, Mrs. Mollie Collins, Daniel B. Horton, Thorbin Sexton, Mattie Gibson, Martha Gibson, Mollie Goins, Flora Goins, Logan Miser, Robert Bales, Brownlow Collins, Frank Gibson, Albert Gibson, Mrs. Albert Gibson, and Fate Miser.

Clay Miser's Sunday school class at Vardy Presbyterian Church in the early 1910s included Mabel Stewart, Eva Mullins, Bessie Odle, Clay Miser, Ola Mae Gibson, my mama,Alyce Horton, Little Alice Collins, and Jane Collins. On the back row are Martha Collins, Mae Miser, Rhoda Mullins, Georgia Collins, Julia Mullins, and Winnie Williams.

The years from 1910 to 1922 added several names. Included are (1910) Miss Mary J. Rankin; (1911) Grace Miser (later married Reverend Taylor), Lillie Ann Miser, Virgie Gibson; (1912) Julia Goins; (1914) Barlow Collins, Roy Miser, May Miser, Nellie Horton, Mrs. Albert Gibson, Wiley Gibson, Hobart Gibson, Sarah Stewart, Winnie Williams, Martha Goins, Herbert Collins; (1915) Ester Collins, Rosa Mullins, Nettie Stewart, Lillie Goins, Carson Stewart, Henley Collins; (1916) Fred Mullins, Pauline Crews, Georgia Collins, Eva Mullins, Rhoda Mullins, Mrs. Ella May Ringley, and Joe Stewart; (1917) Mrs. Carrie Miser, Mrs. Sarah Crews, Bessie Odle, Alyce Horton, Mabel Stewart, Curtis Miser, Edward Miser, Connor Bales, Oppie Miser, Walter Miser, Iowa Williams, Julia Mullins, Mrs. Shelby Williams; (1918) Haines Miser, Grover Mullins, Virgie Horton; (1920) Lee Mullins, Mrs. C. F. Leonard, Frank Miser, Zelma Collins; (1922) Ellen Bales, Olive Bales, Annabelle Miser, Sophia Miser,

Stella Miser, Edith Miser, Ernest Miser, Walter B. Collins, Katy Lee Collins, Helen Stewart, Mary Edith Collins, Vardy Collins (b. 10/24/1908), Jasper Mullins and Mrs. Rhea Saddler (Eliza Goins).

A Vardy young ladies' Sunday school group in the early 1920s.
Front row: an unidentified girl, Sophie Miser, Ellen Bales,
Katy Lee Collins, Lillie Moore, Marjorie Stewart, Edith Miser,
Bonnie Collins, and Nelle Horton.
Back row: Mary Collins, Ellen Stewart, Stella Miser,
Isa Mae Collins, Helen Stewart, Mrs. C. F. Leonard, Ollie Bales,
Rhoda Mullins, Golda Collins, and Joyce Gibson.

The rolls changed again during 1924–1935. The lists include (1924) Rosalie Mullins, Isabelle Horton, Ellen Stewart, Bonnie Collins, and Claude Delph; (1926) Claribel Miser (Horton), Joseph Daniel Stewart, Coby Gibson, Brownlow Mullins, and Eulah Jenkins; (1928) Edna Mullins (Gibson), Ina Mullins, and Hazel Mullins; (1929) Lee Ora Davidson Hasse, and Willa Mae Davidon (Alder); (1931) Mrs. Brownlow Mullins, Mrs. Hughie Mullins, Marshall Davidson, Hughie Mullins, and Harrison Collins; (1933) Drew B. Williams, Alyce Horton Williams, William Grohse, Lillian Grohse, Darnell Williams, Eliza Williams, Belva Williams, and Cynthia (Mrs. Joe) Williams; (1934) Pearl (Mrs. Ernest) Miser, Lucille Collins, Ora Lee Collins, Christine Collins, Ruth Jenkins, Marie Horton, Florence Miser Williams, Ailene Mullins, and Artella Mullins; and (1935) Isa Mae Collins.

The first church book of records began on February 26, 1899, with Noah Collins as the clerk and Rev. J. H. Wallin as the moderator. The last record of the first book is dated April 9, 1935, with Frank Miser as the clerk and Rev. C. F. Leonard as the moderator.

Two other church books of records list members during the church's active service. The October, 1938, through March 31, 1957, "Book of

Records" was kept by Frank Miser until his death, at which time Drew Williams served as clerk with Chester F. Leonard as moderator until 1950. In 1953, the Reverend Charles G. McKarahan became the minister and moderator. The third "Book of Records" from 1959 until 1973 was kept by William P. Grohse, clerk.

Louise Avery wrote to me on January 8, 2004, that the church was active after she left Vardy in 1979. She indicated that "There were still services after that."[8] If books of records were kept after her departure, perhaps the Holston Presbytery has filed them. The ones in my possession are the basis of this chapter's membership lists.

Even though I vowed never to teach, I began my forty-year English teaching career at Gibbs High School in Corryton, Tennessee, following in the footsteps of my parents. During that first year, Fred and I eloped but kept our marriage a secret to avoid teasing by high schoolers.

+ + + + +

Paradox

I didn't wear my religion on my sleeve
And so you thought I hadn't any.
I didn't proclaim Christ as the Savior
So you thought I didn't believe?

I tried to show my religion
By being trusting, compassionate,
Believing, forgiving,
Striving to follow His example.

---

[8]Louise Avery, personal correspondence to DruAnna Overbay, 8 January 2004.

Because I prayed in my heart
You didn't hear my prayer
So you thought I didn't pray?

I didn't talk in tones
Of sternness and seriousness
And wear garments of black
Because I believed that laughing
And wearing colorful clothing
Showed comfort and happiness
With my Lord.

Carrying with me always the guilt of sin,
I could not pretend perfection.
Being imperfect,
I could not condemn others.
So you thought I approved of wrongdoings?

I'm sorry that you did not understand
My religion.
Did I misunderstand yours?

If I say, "I believe in God,
That Jesus Christ is the Savior,"
Speak aloud a prayer,
Talk in tones
Of sternness and seriousness,
Wear garments of black,
Never laugh,
And, most of all,
Condemn others of their sins,
Will you understand
And consider me then a Christian?

Chapter 4

Arrival of Mary J. Rankin

"They came. They stayed. They gave their all," wrote David Swartz in June 2001. The Presbyterian Church, with offices in New York City, began an extensive home missions program in the early 1900s that included, as time went by, "aided fields" in each of the states. In the 1890s Presbyterian representatives on horseback came into the Vardy Community on Blackwater Creek to preach and spend time with some of the families. Two women followed, living in the community for months at a time. However, it was not until 1910 that Scotland-born Mary Rankin, convinced that she should serve the Lord as a Bible reader, teacher, and farmer, came and stayed for three decades.

*Mary J. Rankin
with Isabelle Horton
on Christening Day.*

She had written in her application for home mission service, "I believe that God has called me to the Mountaineers and has been specially preparing me throughout my whole life for work among them." She stated her chief task was "the giving of Christian education with the vocational training that will fit our young people for happier, more useful lives in their home surroundings, and at the same time prepare them for life elsewhere if they should desire to leave here." Miss Rankin remained in Vardy until 1943, when she left to spend her retirement years in Winter Park, Florida.[1]

Even though Miss Rankin had begun living in Florida officially, she found it hard to leave her work at Vardy and returned often during the spring and summer months to help the Leonards with community activities. The VCHS members and families shared vivid memories of her.

Charles Sizemore said, "Coming here as a young woman and staying until she was an old lady illustrated that she dedicated her life to the people in the community. As I look back on it, she was one of the most important persons in my life other than close family. She was my teacher from primer through second grade."[2]

Every time we discuss Miss Rankin, W. C. Collins relates this experience: "A nurse as well as a teacher, she observed our health closely. One example of how well she observed the students is the fact that she noticed that I was malnourished. As a result she arranged for me to stop at various homes on my way to school to drink two glasses of milk every morning."[3]

Constant observation of "her children" made Miss Rankin notice how desperately they needed clothing. She began collecting clothing early in her mission work. "People up north would send clothes to her which she would divide among the children. She made decisions of who needed them the most because we had no money. If it weren't for those clothes, some of us would not even have had coats,"[4] Muhlbauer surmised.

Leonard Gibson adds, "We would go down to Miss Rankin's to look through the coats and shoes. Sometimes we were lucky and found something that we could wear."[5]

Living next door to Miss Rankin made our family even closer to her. Dan Williams, my brother, spoke of her kindness. "She was my first teacher, and I remember that she always had hot chocolate for us in the

---

[1]David F. Swartz, "They Came. They Stayed," manuscript given to Vardy Community Historical Society, June 2001.

[2]Charles Sizemore, Vardy Oral Histories, interviewed by Teresa Burchette, Vardy Church, Sneedville TN, February 2000.

[3]W. C. Collins, personal comments and correspondence to DruAnna Overbay, August 1996–August 2002.

[4]Ruth Jenkins Muhlbauer, Vardy Oral Histories, interviewed by Katie Doman, Baltimore, March 2000, and Vardy Reunion, September 2000.

[5]Leonard Gibson, "Remembering Vardy School," manuscript given to Katie Doman, interviewer, Baltimore, 6 March 2000.

winter. Often she would bake cookies and invite us to have one. I delivered milk to her every day, and she would always have something like cookies or hot chocolate for me."[6]

Her kindness extended throughout the community. Miss Rankin volunteered for other duties, as Muhlbauer explained. "If there were an expectant mother, Miss Rankin was there for her. She helped deliver babies and take care of them during their childhood illnesses. If they got the mumps or the measles, she would go and check on them."[7]

Mary J. Rankin with several of the children whom she delivered while serving the Vardy Community. Those on the front row are Oppie Miser, Claribel Miser, and Mossy Horton.

My sister Margaret Nevels writes, "When and wherever she was needed, she worked as a nurse and midwife to the community. In fact, she delivered me because I came into this world before Dad had time to get the doctor. (We had no telephones in 1937 anywhere in the community.) She would go into the homes to teach people sanitary methods of caring for the sick and how to prevent the spread of disease."[8]

---

[6]Daniel H. Williams, Vardy Oral Histories, interviewed by DruAnna Overbay, Knoxville TN, 15 June 2002.

[7]Muhlbauer.

[8]Margaret Williams Nevels, "Remembering Miss Rankin and Mrs. Leonard," E-mail to DruAnna Overbay, 16 August 2002.

Many others remembered that she had delivered them or their parents. Billie Horton shared, "My mother is the first baby that Miss Rankin delivered in Vardy."[9]

Being one of the last babies Miss Rankin delivered is one of my distinctions. When my dad returned from getting the doctor, Miss Rankin already had me delivered and clean, nursing happily in my mother's arms.

R. C. Mullins reminded me, "Not only did she deliver babies but she stayed long enough to instruct new mothers of their care. Holding a newborn child was a joy contrasted by the sickness and death she had experienced during the flu epidemic of World War I. She worked around the clock, riding on a borrowed mule, going from house to house feeding the sick, giving them medicine, and helping them care for themselves. . . . She was also called upon to dress the dead and speak at funerals. . . . She buried her sadness by finding joy in doing God's work every day. She was instrumental in starting a hot lunch program and night school for adults who could not read or write. Many times she would read articles from farm journals giving farmers knowledge of how to have a better garden. . . . This Presbyterian mission worker who stayed in our community for years played a big role in who I am today. . . . She and the Leonards made sure we were fed, clothed, and healthy; but, of course, they could have left off the codliver oil."[10]

Nevels recalls Miss Rankin's Christian mission, "When I was twelve years old, Miss Rankin asked me to come to her cottage where she discussed the importance of my accepting Jesus as my Savior and the importance of being baptized. She taught Sunday school classes and would read Bible stories to us and relate the importance of the stories to our lives."[11]

The Rankin Cottage

The white frame structure, described as a bungalow, was erected in 1920 with a gable roof but was destroyed during the 1933 tornado. Rebuilding the missionary house meant that the Rankin cottage would look

---

[9]Billie Mullins Horton. Vardy Oral Histories, interviewed by Katie Doman, Sneedville TN, 9 August 2000.

[10]R. C. Mullins, Vardy Oral Histories, interviewed by DruAnna Overbay, Morristown TN, 15 June 2002.

[11]Nevels, "Remembering Miss Rankin and Mrs. Leonard."

more like the other campus buildings. Described as having eight buildings during that time period, the Presbyterian property included not only the church house, manse, and school but also the clinic, summer house, garage, and chicken house as well as the Rankin Cottage. Two other buildings that may have been included were the well house and hothouse. Surely the outdoor toilets were not included in that count. All with the exception of the church house and manse had corrugated metal siding. These buildings were erected under the direction of Mr. William H. Leonard, the Reverend Chester F. Leonard's father. When the Leonards went there, the Center consisted of only a church, the 1902 school, and a mission house.

Miss Rankin not only promoted and presented the Gospel but worked diligently to promote Christian principles through her daily activities.

The Rankin Cottage, located to the left of the church, is built on a rock foundation. The cottage has four large rooms. To the left of the living room is a bedroom. The kitchen, which is behind the living room, also has a bedroom to its left. From the kitchen's back door, one goes to the back porch, which also serves as the entry to the cellar/dairy dug into the adjacent hillside. Wooden steps lead to the attic, which is large enough for six to ten guests to sleep on rollaway cots. Miss Rankin used this area to store the boxes of clothing that were sent to the community.

When asked about the boxes of clothing, Dave Swartz replied, "I don't remember the attic section. I guess I was up there, but all I remember was the downstairs area. We had electricity there and cold water coming into the kitchen sink. We had two stoves: one for coal and one for wood."[12] Dark hardwood floors and paneling completed the decor. The house had gray metal siding trimmed in white to match the other campus buildings; however, the structure is now white.

Behind her house was a large garden spot where Mr. Leonard planted vegetables. In the front were English walnut trees, a butternut tree, and dogwood trees. Creeping rose bushes climbed the fence that separated the church property from my parents' property and kept the sheep contained. A gate opened the path between the two homes, and Miss Rankin used the outdoor toilets behind the church.

When I was in the second grade, my mother was also my teacher.

+ + + + +

Cookies Baking

Slipping through the fence
My red tuliped pocket snagged and ripped
Grass stained the white dress tail
Sheep's in the meadow
"Little girl, crying
Come blow your nose!"

Scooping me in her comforting arms
Miss Rankin carried me
Into her kitchen's

---

[12]David F. Swartz, Vardy Oral Histories, interviewed by DruAnna Overbay, Boone NC, 5 June 1999.

Aroma of baking cookies
Being made for tomorrow's
Sunday School Class.

She rocked me until my tears dried
And then she stiched my tulip pockets
Onto my new Easter dress
And washed away the stains.

"Jesus loves me, this I know,"
She sang me to sleep
And pressed the dampness away.

When I awoke, she took my hand,
Led me through the garden gate home
So Mama wouldn't spank me.

(My first memory of Miss Rankin)

Chapter 5

Chester F. Leonard's Leadership

Miss Rankin's mission work paved the way for Chester F. Leonard's ministry and community involvement in Vardy. They made an unusual team with a similar sense of missionary service: "You shall love the Lord your God . . . and your neighbor as yourself" (Luke 10:27). Both believed in the potential of adults and especially the children, "to increase in wisdom and in stature and in favor with God and man" (Luke 2:52).[1]

This picture of Chester F. Leonard was made when he was a student at McCormick Seminary and was sent to Josephine Wicks during their courtship.

Mr. Leonard is described by David F. Swartz as a "can do" man, who after three years in the field, wrote, "We have a wonderful opportunity here to use everything that we have ever learned and to try out some things that we have hardly dared think about before. . . . During our brief stay in Vardy, we have built our house, leveled a lawn from the mountain side, blasted rock and hauled wood and scraped for a playground, taught school, operated a moving-picture machine, held classes in woodworking, fought against moonshine and, best of all, had the chance to preach and teach the Gospel of Christ every Sabbath and several times a week."[2]

When asked, just before the new school was built in 1929, where he expected the children to live as adults, Mr. Leonard responded, "We do not beg them to stay, and we do not force them to leave. If they remain among

[1]David F. Swartz, "They Came. They Stayed," manuscript given to Vardy Community Historical Society, June 2001.

[2]Chester F. Leonard, journal notations (1921–1946), given to David F. Swartz.

us, we shall have provided leaders that will take the next generation another step or two up the ladder of progress. If they leave us and go into the other parts of the world, as we hope many of them will do, they will be better equipped to do their share of the world's work and to help others in their religious and social life. They will not be handicapped by an early stunting of vision and life. They will see their new surroundings as they really are and be able to help in making them what they should be. We are trying to produce a normal-minded community of people with the desire, the will, and the ability to live the more abundant life wherever they may be."[3]

Mary Rankin (left) visited with Josephine and Chester Leonard shortly after the completion of their new home, presently known as the C. F. Leonard Manse.

"I came to Vardy in 1946, on a one-year internship between my second and third year of seminary," explained Swartz. "Miss Rankin had left. I lived in her house. I found Mr. Leonard, my supervisor, determined, disciplined, and demanding. Demanding one's best—his and yours! I was in awe of his knowledge and abilities, believing him to have a photographic memory. He told others long before I arrived that he liked the job at Vardy because, 'In no other place does one have a better opportunity to prove oneself an all-around man.' "[4]

From ages fourteen to sixteen, Mr. Leonard worked as an apprentice mechanic for the Chicago Brass Company of Kenosha, Wisconsin. In the next five years, up to his twenty-first birthday, he continued as a mechanic

---

[3]Leonard, personal correspondence to David F. Swartz.
[4]Swartz, "They Came. They Stayed."

but also sold mattresses for a company in Birmingham, Alabama. He had no high school diploma but was accepted as a "conditional freshman applicant" at Maryville College in Tennessee. He graduated magna cum laude in the class of 1917 and entered seminary in Chicago the fall. He worked in the Vardy program two summers before graduating from McCormick Seminary in the spring of 1920. Mr. Leonard signed an agreement with the Board of Home Missions of the Presbyterian Church as the pastor of a Demonstration Parish Plan for a seven-year term beginning May 1, 1920. This agreement stated that "Vardy shall provisionally concern itself, besides evangelism and worship, with rural schools, good roads, public health improvement, recreation, and economic betterment of all who dwell in Vardy."

Public health improvement was a constant concern for Miss Rankin and Mr. Leonard. During World War I, the pervasive flu epidemic did not spare Vardy. Miss Rankin learned about treatment from the *American Journal of Medicine*. To combat illnesses which were often a combination of hookworm, flu, and goiter, the health department in Nashville gave her permission to dispense medicine. The news of her successful work spread to Dr. Otto of Johns Hopkins University, who came to study her program. Her program was soon written about in medical journals. After a sabbatical leave spent in New York City, Miss Rankin was awarded an M.A. degree by Columbia University in 1920.[5]

In 1926 Mr. Leonard went to Johns Hopkins to study public health. Swartz continued:

> He told me he did not get an advanced degree because he didn't want to waste his time writing a dissertation! I was impressed with the medical supplies . . . Mr. Leonard had in the dispensary building behind the manse to which the school children felt welcome. Mrs. Leonard wrote shortly after her husband's death: "He loved his first aid work with the children and was proud of this incident. A little girl came to him with a bad burn. He asked why she had not come earlier, and she replied, 'Did not want to bother you.' The preacher told her, 'I am not bothered.' The child replied, 'Preacher, my mommie says, if you were not here, we'd just have

---

[5]Swartz, "They Came. They Stayed."

to let our hurts go.' He contended that our community had many hurts."[6]

As Chester F. Leonard surveys the site of the future school,
his wife Josephine enjoys a sandwich from their picnic.

Soon after the completion of the new school building, Mr. Leonard took his vacation and study leave in 1930 to pursue courses in generators and motors at the Nashville School of Mechanics. Vardy's electrical system with a generator and many of the shop tools in the vocational training program for the boys were installed and maintained by Leonard, who knew about the uses of electricity for light, heat, and motion.

Mr. Leonard never ended his quest for knowledge. The question arose why so few snake handlers in area religious services were bitten. He corresponded with herpetologists at the Brookline Zoo in Boston. He was told that snakes, when held in the air, tend to be disoriented and seldom bite and, when placed in an enclosure and provoked, expel some of their venom.

Travel slides or sound movies were shown in the school auditorium on nights when the moon was full, allowing for easier, safer walking. *National Geographic* was a favorite magazine for the older children studying geography. Mr. Leonard told of a written agreement with the editors of that magazine to allow Eastman Kodak to make colored slides of requested pictures from the *National Geographic* for classroom use in Vardy.

---

[6]Swartz, "They Came. They Stayed."

"As much as Mr. Leonard relied on visual aids to teach and entertain, I never saw him with a camera. In a personal information form for the Presbyterian Mission Board, completed in April of 1947, while I was living in Vardy, Mr. Leonard checked thirty-three of forty-two possible skills. Such knowledge and experience were considered valuable for the missionary programs. Photography was not checked. Even though we are sure that the photographs that were taken and are now displayed in the church/museum were a result of Mr. Leonard's encouragement, I think it unlikely that they were taken by Mr. Leonard."[7]

Dave Swartz, who had spent his ministerial internship at Vardy during the 1940s, returned to the valley during the 1998 reunion and became one of the active board members. Those who went to Vardy during the time he was there have always remembered his friendship and the fun that he provided because of his knowledge of audio-video equipment. He helped preserve their cultural history by making movies of the people and their activities around their homes, at the Vardy School, and at the Vardy Church. Fifty-six years later, copies of those movies are still being enjoyed by those who were filmed.

Swartz added that "As a prospective minister with a couple of courses in sermon preparation under my belt, I listened to Mr. Leonard's sermons and to his talks for school programs. Never did I hear an uninteresting or poorly prepared speech. He retired early after supper and read for hours." His sermons were written out in full although some of the school talks are in outline form. We are fortunate that Chester Leonard gave copies of his sermons to one of the VCHS board members."[8]

Following Mr. Leonard's death, Swartz wrote to Mrs. Leonard, "Mr. Leonard helped me in many, many ways in preparing me for rural work: in giving me a sense of duty and discipline; in exhibiting a love for all kinds

---

[7]Swartz, "They Came. They Stayed."

[8]David F. Swartz, Vardy Oral Histories, interviewed by DruAnna Overbay, Boone NC, 5 June 1999.

of Christian service; and in showing me a devotion to a people. I hope I can follow part of the distance along the path . . . he trod."[9]

Katie Doman concluded that:

> Preacher Leonard, who served the community as both minister and teacher, included in his progressive and practical curriculum everything he could think of that his students might need. He and his family members, who included his wife Josephine and parents William and Florence Leonard [incorrectly identified: Florence was a sister; Ida was "Mother"], gave lessons in hygiene, etiquette, and health care. The school offered academic instruction and resources, spiritual and moral guidance, hot lunches, and playgrounds for physical fitness. He also included what many of those interviewed still refer to as "manual training" in areas such as agriculture, carpentry, and other hands-on fields, partially because he realized that many students might choose to end their education after they finished at Vardy. He wanted to send students out prepared for every possible path they chose.
>
> The school often opened after hours to provide educational opportunities for adults and to serve as a community center for social events such as softball games and holiday dinners. Preacher Leonard succeeded in his goal—former students have used the training and education they received to succeed in careers in construction, education, law, retail, farming, and a number of other areas.[10]

The tenure of Preacher Leonard, as we in Vardy fondly called him, is recorded in the Vardy Community Presbyterian Church records. The second entry in the church records after Preacher Leonard had become the new minister records the first members of the church to join:

> On Sunday, September 5, 1920, at the Vardy Presbyterian Church the following persons were received by the Session & examined: Mrs. C. F. Leonard by letter from the Fifth Avenue Church, B'ham, Ala. Miss Zelma Collins, Mr. Lee Mullins, & Mr. Frank Miser on confirmation of Faith. Miss Zelma Collins & Mr.

---

[9]Swartz, personal correspondence to Josephine Leonard, June 1952.

[10]Katie Doman, manuscript submitted to *Windows on the Past*, 20 June 2002.

Miser having been baptized, the four were received in the church at the morning service & received their first Communion with us.

C.F. Leonard, Evan.
N.T. Collins, Clerk[11]

Reverend Leonard takes a break from his busy schedule to relax with Brownie, a neighbor's dog.

Preacher Leonard continued his work at Vardy until the end of October 1951. Prior to that time, however, he had written two letters to the officers and members of the church stating his intentions of leaving. The first letter is dated September 14, 1947, the second, April 15, 1948. Heartwrenching as it is, the letter begins:

This is to notify you that the resignation of Chester F. Leonard, presented to you long ago, at this date becomes effective.

The doctor has repeatedly warned me that I must stop work for a time. For three years I have not heeded that warning and now I have come to the place that I cannot more add to your welfare; in fact, I can hardly get to the services. I have promised that when the time came that I could no more help you, at that time I would leave this great field of wonderfully fine folks open to someone who can help.

---

[11]Noah Collins, Vardy Community Presbyterian Church Records, Vardy TN, 1920.

After careful examination of x-rays, cardiogram records, etc., I have been told that I must get away from all climbing, every physical and emotional disturbance, and all responsibility, if I ever expect to be able to serve, or even live.

Therefore, I am leaving you. I am sorry that I cannot say: GOODBYE, but that will take too much of my strength and hurt too much. As you know, I have loved all of you as if you belonged to my family. I know how Jesus felt when He wept and said: I WOULD HAVE GATHERED YOU AS A HEN GATHERS TOGETHER HER CHICKENS to protect and to help; but I could not because many have not wanted what I could offer, May the Lord keep every one of you and give to you those blessings that are best for you. . . .

Thank all of you who have tried to make my work as easy as possible. Thank all of you who have tried to cooperate during these past many years in giving this community the opportunity to be its best. I have given the best of my life to you and many of you have been much blessed. Your community is happier, healthier and (I believe) more like Jesus wishes it to be than it was thirty years ago. l am sorry that, with God's help, it could not have become an even happier, better place for your children.

May God bless all of you and keep you close to Himself,
Your friend and former minister,

Chester F. Leonard[12]

It is never easy to give up one who was and continues to be as loved as Preacher Leonard. In a tearful meeting of the church on April 18, 1948, the session would not allow the resignation of the reverend. The body then decided to petition for help from Dr. Randolph (Presbyterian Board of National Missions) in having Mr. Leonard return to Vardy when his health permitted. The petitions, motions, and discussions continued with no real action taken. In truth, nobody wanted the Leonards to leave.

On October 10, 1948, other members stepped forward to help in church and community activities. These included Jean Sizemore, Beatrice Trent, Claude Collins, Luigene Williams, Mrs. Mary Grohse, and Roxy Davidson.

---

[12]Chester F. Leonard, second resignation letter to Congregation, 15 April 1948.

Then, on February 6, 1949, Reverend C. F. Leonard was asked to assume limited work, depending on his health. The limited work included leading the regular church worship, being singing director, organist, and Bible teacher at the school, and taking charge of the school assembly program. The work of Preacher Leonard continued until 1951. The church record states:

> Meeting of the Session—Sunday, Sept 30, 1951.
> A meeting was called of the Session by Mrs. C. F. Leonard because of the illness of the Moderator C. F. Leonard. D. B. Williams was elected Moderator Pro Tem and the meeting was called to order with the opening prayer by the Moderator Pro Tem. After the opening prayer, Mrs. C. F. Leonard told us that she and Rev. C. F. Leonard and Father Leonard were leaving the last of October because of the Rev. Leonard's health.[13]

Several of the community leaders carried on his work. Drew B. Williams, moderator, W. P. Grohse, Jr., clerk, and other elders and deacons Darnell Williams, Eliza Goins, Herbert Collins, and William Grohse, Sr., as well as Anderson Bell, Ed Williams, Stella Miser, Alyce Williams, Dana Johnson, Lillian Grobse, and Cecil Miser were instrumental in continuing the church services. The Leonards came and went in the manse. During the summer from July to September 10, 1948, the Reverend and Mrs. Fitzhugh Dotson lived in the Rankin cottage and helped with services.

---

[13]Vardy Community Presbyterian Church Records, Vardy TN.

Clay and Carrie Miser are pictured on their wedding day. They continued to live in Vardy, where they were active members of the Presbyterian Church.

+ + + + +

Pink Cameo

White-faced Gibson girl
On your shoulder
Pinned a three rose corsage
Trinity symbolized
On your scooped neck gown
Silver filigree encircling your aura of pink
Holding you in my hand
Groom's words hiding in letters
Declaring his love
Whispered in the bride's ear again.
What was said that night
When you were placed in her care?

(Chester Leonard's wedding night gift to Josephine
bequeathed to Mama, given to me.)

Chapter 6   The Preacher's Wife

Born in Paducah, Kentucky, on March 18, 1894, Josephine Wicks married
Chester F. Leonard on December 25, 1918, in the Birmingham, Alabama,
Sixth Avenue Presbyterian Church, where she was a member. Whether she
met him in Birmingham or while a student at Maryville College is unclear.
He was an assistant librarian at Maryville, where she also worked and had
gone to school.

*Seated on the front steps of the manse
are Miss Rankin and Mr. and Mrs.
Leonard. Miss Rankin had greeted
the Leonards when they came to Vardy.
Now they were saying goodbye to her
as she leaves Vardy for the winter
in Florida.*

A personal information form completed for the Board of National
Missions of the Presbyterian Church USA by Mr. Leonard on July 5, 1947,
lists his wife's occupation as stenographer. Certainly while at Vardy, she
served the church and the school in that capacity. Her education is listed as
high school and college.

In personal correspondence to David F. Swartz, Mrs. Leonard wrote,
"I do not have the necessary degrees now required for teaching. After two
years of college, I had one year of kindergarten training in Chicago, one
year of training in a school for recreational leaders in Baltimore and a
spring term at Peabody in Nashville. I did not bother to save one single
credit."[1]

Those who remembered Mrs. Leonard described her in various ways.
"[S]he is in one day a wife, teacher, organizer, housekeeper, cook . . .
encourager, appreciator, general spreader of sweetness and light, diplomat,

---

[1]Josephine Leonard, personal correspondence to David F. Swartz, 9 July 1952.

and if need should arise, a 'little fighter' who would do credit to any commando," Amelia Barr Elmore wrote.[2] Years later two Maryville graduates who remembered having met her described her as a "feisty lady."[3]

Her feisty personality was tempered by a sweetness described as her being "a real nice person." Charles Sizemore stated, "When Jean, my sister, and I brought milk to her in the evenings, she would give us a treat for bringing it."[4]

However, Dan Williams remembered that she usually sent a piece of lemon meringue pie home to his father, while admonishing him not to eat it. Having not forgotten that she offered him no pie, Dan said, "I was just a kid, and that really hurt my feelings."[5]

"She was generous in asking me over to eat. Sometimes she'd ask me if I wanted to bring something to add to the meal . . . and she wouldn't use it. I thought that was unusual. But there was always good food, and we did share in that way," Swartz added.[6]

Cleland Collins remembered that "Mrs. Leonard was a very nice lady of slight build. She was very pleasant, and it was obvious that she liked the people of Vardy. She was the church and school librarian and was very interested in the children and their education."[7]

Margaret Nevels writes, "Mrs. Leonard kept busy around the manse, school, and church by promoting the activities of the church and school. While I was in school, she came each week to present a program for an assembly of all of the schoolchildren. She usually read us a story, sometimes from *Aesop's Fables* or *Uncle Remus Tales*. She put a lot of expression and voice variations in her reading, which made the stories come alive to us. She would discuss the virtue or the moral of the story

---

[2]Amelia Barr Elmore, "Family Portrait," *The Church on the Hill*, Englewood Cliffs NJ, January 1943.

[3]David F. Swartz, Vardy Oral Histories, interviewed by DruAnna Overbay, Boone NC, 5 June 1999.

[4]Charles Sizemore, Vardy Oral Histories, interviewed by Teresa Burchette, Vardy Church, Sneedville TN, February 2000.

[5]Daniel H. Williams, Vardy Oral Histories, interviewed by DruAnna Overbay, Knoxville TN, 15 June 2002.

[6]Swartz, "They Came, They Stayed."

[7]Cleland Collins, Vardy Oral Histories, interviewed by Sally Collins and DruAnna Overbay, Morristown TN, 25 April 1999.

after she had read, and then she would ask us questions to get us thinking about the virtue."[8]

A favorite collection of stories was *The Jack Tales* that were so familiar to many children in the Appalachian Mountains. Asking Mrs. Leonard about *The Jack Tales*, David Swartz received the following note in June, 1971: "Don't expect me to render any *Jack Tales*. I gave two volumes to the Hayden Lasters when I left Tennessee. I have one treasured story— 'How the Willopus Wallopus Came to Sour Apple Cove.' "[9]

Children could check out these colorfully illustrated books from the church library, but they could not check out textbooks. Since books were not free, several remembered working for Mrs. Leonard to earn money to purchase them. According to Claribel Horton, "She had a little bag of money that she kept behind the locked door leading to the attic. When it was time to pay the other children, she always sent me to get her moneybag. I was the only one who knew where she hid her money. Sometimes she told me to get a nickel or dime to pay myself because she trusted me. I also ironed for her and made biscuits, cakes, and pies when I went to Vardy."[10]

Another Vardy student, Ruth Jenkins Muhlbauer, told me she worked for Mrs. Leonard for eight years. "That is how I got money to buy clothing for school," she said. "She [Mrs. Leonard] paid me eight cents an hour. I started working for her when I was ten or eleven by washing dishes, carrying wood, or helping with the laundry. As a result, I could pay for my uniform when I went to boarding school."[11]

"Working for Mrs. Leonard, I learned how to make a bed correctly," Mae Williams Sexton stated. "She was a very particular housekeeper, and everything had to be done just right. I did her washing, ironing, and mopping, beginning when I was a sophomore at Hancock County High School. I was so happy the first time she paid me because she gave me a quarter, which was a little more than the seven cents an hour that she owed me; but it was just enough to buy a tube of Tangee lipstick that she knew

---

[8]Margaret Williams Nevels, "Remembering Miss Rankin and Mrs. Leonard," e-mail to DruAnna Overbay, 16 August 2002.

[9]Josephine Leonard, correspondence with David Swartz, June 1971.

[10]Claribel Horton. Vardy Oral Histories, interviewed by DruAnna Overbay, Seymour IN, August 1999.

[11]Ruth Jenkins Muhlbauer, telephone interview.

I really wanted since all of the other high school girls were wearing that color."[12]

Sexton's aunt, Eula Mullins, said, "One thing that I will always remember about Mrs. Leonard was the way she sang in church. It was really funny to hear her warbling high voice. We used to go around the school trying to sing like her just for fun."[13]

At the Vardy School reunion in 2004, Glessie Collins Cummins wrote, "When I hear the national anthem, I remember Mrs. Leonard singing this song in the assembly room during programs. Even today, tears come in my eyes and I feel very proud to be a free American hearing that song. Of course, I'm always reminded of Mrs. Leonard's singing soprano."[14]

After their departure from Vardy Miss Rankin and Mrs. Leonard returned often to visit with friends.

In addition to her unusual voice, the exotic flowers that she grew in her hothouse were the talk of the students. Cacti and other flowers, not native to Vardy, flourished in her care. She also had a beautiful flower garden below the manse where daffodils, sweet peas, and tiger lilies still bloom

[12]Mae Williams Sexton, Vardy Oral Histories, interviewed by Troy Lee Williams, Laurel MD, 28 September 1999.

[13]Eula Mullins, Vardy Oral Histories, interviewed by Katie Doman, Baltimore MD, March 2000.

[14]Glessie Collins Cummings, Vardy Community School Questionnaire, 4 September 2004.

from her initial plantings. Swartz remembered that "She did have some nice flowers."[15] And Muhlbauer recalled, "When I worked for the Leonards, I would go out on Sunday mornings and help her pick them, and she would arrange them in vases on her back porch. I would carry them over to the church and put them in front of the pulpit or on the communion table."[16]

Having no children of her own, Mrs. Leonard made us her children. If we needed scolding, she told our parents. When I went off to Warren Wilson, she sent the college money designated for Vardy students' use. My cousins and I were surprised with a few extra dollars every now and then. At that age, I don't think I appreciated it as much as I should have. My mother would often ask if I had written a thank-you note.

Mrs. Leonard wrote Dave Swartz in May, 1971: "My once home church in Chattanooga is having its hundredth anniversary and would like to have some of its people who went into church work be there. I do not know how this would work out, as I still feel more close to the Birmingham church. I'd feel like an antique at such a reunion as I joined when I was 16."[17]

After Mr. Leonard's death, Mrs. Leonard moved to a retirement home in Pasadena, California, for widowed wives of ministers. There Fred Wills interviewed her on May 1, 1979. The Presbyterian Historical Society in Philadelphia houses the cassette recording of her oral history. Unfortunately, the VCHS was unable to obtain permission for its use.

Corresponding with and visiting Vardy friends as long as she was able, Mrs. Leonard maintained her residence in California until her death in 1982.

In one of Mrs. Leonard's letters to Margaret Nevels, she revealed that she had written a short story based on a remembrance that Miss Rankin had shared with her concerning the community's celebration of Christmas when Miss Rankin first went there. Mrs. Leonard sent a copy of the story to Margaret. That story, which was read to Mrs. Leonard's friends at the retirement home, is reprinted on the following page.

---

[15]Swartz, "They Came, They Stayed."

[16]Muhlbauer, Vardy Oral Histories.

[17]Josephine Leonard, personal correspondence to David Swartz, May 1971.

Josephine Leonard's good-humored fun found expression in many ways, including her hat decorations, which won "best in show" at the retirement home in which she lived.

Vardy's First Christmas Decorations
by Josephine Leonard

It was Christmas Eve in 1910 in the narrow Vardy Valley, where I was later to live for more than 30 years. There was a swell of feeling rising like a glad tide over the outside world, but here there might be drinking and shooting. As a counter attraction, the Missionary Woman wanted to keep Christmas with a tree and gifts from churches in far-off cities, thus emphasizing the true way to keep the festival of the Christ-child.

How to avoid trouble beforehand was the problem. Her people had never heard of decorating their small homes on the outside, but at her suggestion, they went at it with a will. Each house was flanked with green boughs, and these hung with scraps of paper, bits of cloth, tin tobacco signs, anything with color. Three small prizes were offered for the most attractive trimming.

One enthusiastic woman worked two days and two nights without taking off her clothes to make old newspapers into trimmings, snipping the whole night thru by the light from her hearth. The art child of her brain was a rose formed of three paper discs of descending sizes, notched around the edges and fastened flat one upon the other.

Sukey commented, "While I set there a-workin', I'd git so happy that I'd find myself a-mumblin' and a-singin'. And a-laughin' and a-shoutin' to myself."

An old woman came walking down the valley to "take Christmas" with her folks. "Sakes" she cried, "What's took Blackwater?"

Aunt Hiley Ann replied with lofty unconcern, "Oh, we're just a-prettyin' up for Christmas."

A man riding thru the Valley carried the news that he even met an old hog running down the road with a twig "a-stickin' outta each ear."

By this time not a soul in the community would have gotten drunk, feeling that he was setting the whole county an example. Since only a mountain man could set a relative value on the decorations, three of them set out as judges. The young men gathered at the churchhouse to hang the gifts. They hung the walls with greens, and a whole gleaming holly tree stood ready for its load of wonderful presents.

The Missionary Woman heard a commotion and ran to see a democratic throng going to meet the judges. The group included men, women, children, hunting dogs giving quick yaps of excitement, two nervous hens squawking in terror and Miss Rankin (a cow named for the Missionary Woman) in the center joyously switching her tail. There were shouts of merriment and the punctuation blare of a tin horn, and somewhere down the road the ringing of a farm bell broke in.

Sukey said, "I wuz never so happy in all my life. I jest wanted to yell, but I thot' everybody'd think I'd gone plumb crazy, so I choked and swallered it down till I thot I'd bust. Then I heerd the bells a-ringin'. An' I sed, 'Childern, we ain't got no bell to ring, but let's sing her. So we sung her, 'O the Heaven Bells Is Ringing'. SING. Childern, sing! SING, or I'll bust my bosom! It jest fitted the 'casion and before I know'd it, I wuz aflappin' my arms and a-shoutin'.

"When Uncle Lonnie came a-ridin' along with the flag, his face just shone as if he will never face it to the world agin. Childern, oh, the heaven bells is a-ringin'. 'When I heerd that horn, I sed, 'That's Gabriel a-blarin' his trumpet. Seems like this place is just heaven, and he's a-blowin' his horn. Shure, the Lord is here this day. He is right here a-walkin' up and down the road. Childern, why shouldn't He be here as well as anywheres else?

In the church house, lighted candles glittered on the holly tree with its load of red berries and gifts. Santa held sway until the time came to close with carols, the first ever sung in that little church. The strength of these venerable songs is in their objectiveness. The people really saw the guiding star as it journeyed from afar. If it were trip by muleback over mountain roads, what matter so long as they brought the true gifts of the spirit of the newborn King?

"Once in royal David's city
Stood a lowly cattle shed,
Where a mother laid her Baby
In a manger for His bed."

To them it was no tradition dulled by repetition; it was a fact. They knew from their own experience the insufficiency of such shelter. They heard the rustle of the fodder and the slow munching of the cattle in the dark. They knew the pain and the joy of it.

"And His shelter was a stable,
And His cradle was a stall.

Sukey was right. The Lord did walk up and down their road that day. And life ever after was different to those who heard the sound of His garments as He passed.[18]

---

[18]Josephine Leonard, "Vardy's First Christmas," given to Margaret Williams Nevels, June 1971.

Chapter 7

The Manse

The Leonards built the manse around 1921 after the original 1902 manse was destroyed by fire. It is a one-story frame bungalow which, in the 1920s, was featured in the Sears-Roebuck catalog. The prefabricated and precut plan 550 was ordered from the Lumber Company of Davenport, Iowa. Prepackaged building parts were shipped by rail to Ben Hur, Virginia, where Chester F. Leonard and a group of community neighbors hauled it section by section in a wagon drawn by a team of mules.

An aerial view of the manse and clinic shows
the deterioration that had occurrred
before the 1998 restoration of the property.

A recessed portico features a dark wood doorway with a transom and sidelights, considered high style for its time period. Roofed with cedar shakes, which extend to the eaves and just below the attic, the manse has wood lapped siding which complements the decor. Originally painted to match the church, the manse has undergone a number of updated colors and roof compositions.

A fieldstone walk took visitors to steps onto a covered front porch. The door opened into a spacious living room. To the left of the living room was Mrs. Leonard's bedroom, which had a closet. One also entered the dining room through a double doorway in the living room. Mr. Leonard's bedroom was entered on the left of the dining room. The two bedrooms were joined by a connecting bath. David F. Swartz added, "They had separate bedrooms, I recall."[1]

From stairs in Mr. Leonard's bedroom, one entered the attic. To the right of the dining room was the kitchen. A covered back porch with large windows across the manse's length was added during the school construction. Here Mr. Leonard had made a library and study area for reading.

"I always went in the back door. I don't really remember going in the front door. It was quicker to where the food was. . . . He had some marvelous books in his study and wanted me to read certain books. . . . Books that an older person wants you to read are probably books that you don't want to read. . . . So, I didn't really read the books that he suggested. . . . But he had marvelous magazines such as *Arizona Highways* and *National Geographic*."[2]

The sparsely decorated home featured a window seat beneath the front double windows of the living room, which had another set of double windows on the right. "When it was too cold or snowy to walk home to Newman's Ridge, I would spend the night with the Leonards and sleep on that window seat. It suited me just fine, and the padding on it was very comfortable. At least, I don't remember it not being. I stayed warm all night because the wood stove was right across the living room from me."[3]

Cross ventilation was the key to cooling in the summer; therefore, windows were plentiful for light and air. Mrs. Leonard's bedroom had large double windows in the front that were opposite Mr. Leonard's window on the back. "When each bedroom's bathroom doors were open, the breeze was wonderful,"[4] Claribel Horton said. Large double windows were also in the kitchen and dining room.

Oakey Collins told me, "Father Leonard's woodworking boys built the storage cabinets in the kitchen, and they also built a corner china cabinet. Cleland and I both helped build those along with our cousin Pet Collins."[5]

---

[1]David F. Swartz, Vardy Oral Histories, interviewed by DruAnna Overbay, Boone NC, 5 June 1999.

[2]Swartz, Vardy Oral Histories.

[3]W. C. Collins, personal comments and correspondence to DruAnna W. Overbay, August 1996–August 2002.

[4]Claribel Miser Horton, Vardy Oral Histories, interviewed by DruAnna W. Overbay, Seymour IN, 17 July 1999.

[5]Oakey Hendrix Collins, Vardy Oral Histories, interviewed by Sally Collins and DruAnna Overbay, Morristown TN, 25 April 1999.

For the 1920s the wallpaper was very stylish. Each room and the ten-foot ceilings were papered, often featuring a flower design for the walls and a complementary scroll or triangled-dot design on the ceiling. Beaded boards at a height of four feet surrounded the walls of the bathroom and kitchen.

The bathroom contained an enameled tub with feet. The toilet's water tank was high above the bowl, and a sink skirted with rose-patterned material was on the right wall beneath a mirrored medicine cabinet. Over the cabinet was a porcelain light fixture with an electrical outlet. A cistern provided water.

Hardwood flooring was throughout the manse. Each room had a schoolhouse light in the ceiling as well as one electrical outlet located high on the wall.

Furniture given as wedding presents had been saved from the fire's destruction. My grandparents Daniel Boone Horton and Adelaide's dining room gift, purchased from Montgomery Ward in Middlesboro, was given to Alyce Williams when the last missionary, Louise Avery, left. It has a buffet, a large round table with two leaves, and six chairs. Other gifts included Mr. Leonard's living room rocking chair, Mrs. Leonard's bedroom rocking chair, a straight back chair, a dry sink, and a desk. These items remained in the house until the last missionary left. Louise Avery honored Mrs. Leonard's will by making sure each named recipient received the furniture specifically left to him. These items were given to members of the families who had given them as gifts to the Leonards through the years.

Behind the manse is the famed clinic, which sat atop the Leonard's cellar. Treatment was administered in one long room where medical records of those served were also filed. The adjacent long room, considered the church study, was a storage area for church and Sunday school supplies. Storage boxes full of slides were stacked on the shelves along with Bible school literature. A large desk occupied the far end.

*The homeplaces of
Adelaide Collins Horton,
Nancy Collins Miser,
and their mother Cynthia Collins
were all located near
the Vardy Community Center.*

+ + + + +

Melungeon Ancestry

My mother handed me a legacy
of old family portraits,
Though I'm not sure what she intended me to
do with them.

I held them fast in my heart and dreams until
the names of those who were
Are as familiar to me
As those who are.

As I assemble this littany
I wonder if anything of my life
or my name will ever become
As familiar to one of my descendants?

Vardemon Collins and Spanish Peggy
Alfred Collins, Elizabeth Mullins (James Mullins, Clara Martin)

Simeon Collins, Frankie Bunch (Benjamin Bunch, Mary Dotson)
Grandpa Batey Collins, Grandma Cynthia,
Pappa Daniel Horton, Adelaide Collins,
Mama Alyce Horton and Daddy Drew Willams.

You call to me down the ages
To restore the family pride
A pride of what these people accomplished
As they set out to educate and carve
A place to call home
You push me to restore
what little is left of our legacy.

(While scrapbooking the family pictures.)

Chapter 8

The Clinic

When it was recognized that there was a tendency within the community for the occurrence of certain diseases resulting from malnutrition, Reverend Leonard and Miss Rankin began to explore the possibilities of how to help. They began clinics in the church and at the new school.

A reflection of these health-related activities is found in Chester F. Leonard's annual reports. "Our health record work for the year of 1930 has been interesting. We have carried on the regular education that has been going on for years. Besides, considerable medicine has been distributed, lunches have been given to the smaller children, and clinics have been held. I mention specifically the program for the elimination of worms and the clinic for the prevention of trachoma, including the crowded busload of people who went to Knoxville to be examined and treated."[1]

Unfortunately, Preacher Leonard and Miss Rankin were not always able to help those who had complications from childhood diseases. The notations on the back of this photograph read, "Irene [fourth from the left] died with aftereffects of measles."

An all too common malady was worms. Round worms, hookworms, and pin worms were commonly found in the children's systems because so many went barefoot and did not wash their hands or foods properly. Ruth

[1]Chester F. Leonard, "Annual Reports," Vardy Community Presbyterian Church Records, 1930.

Jenkins Muhlbauer related, "Every year we had to take a stool specimen to the clinic to be checked for worms. If anyone had worms, then Mr. Leonard prescribed a treatment."[2]

An effort to teach the people proper hygiene included giving toothbrushes and toothpaste to the residents. When lye soap supplies ran low, Preacher Leonard suggested that the lye soap be kept for washing clothing and bed linens, and he distributed donated toiletries. Muhlbauer remembered, "We didn't brush our teeth before then. We would clean our teeth by chewing on a willow switch with the leaves still on it. Really, it did taste good and did a fairly good job."[3]

During December 1932 two clinics were held for those who needed to have teeth removed. "A total of eighty-seven were examined, mostly schoolchildren. Several teeth were extracted. Advice was given to others as to the care of their teeth. If that advice is followed, I am sure that the clinics were worthwhile. In our clinics last season, we had a young doctor, who we thought would be just the man for our kind of work here. We did all that we could to retain him, but for some reason he moved from the county, and we are again looking for a doctor upon whom we can depend in our times of need."[4]

Lloyd Williams recalled, "There wasn't a doctor in Vardy so we depended on Preacher Leonard or Miss Rankin to take care of us."[5]

The 1934 report showed a concern for the typhoid and diphtheria epidemics spreading throughout the nation: "The clinics for the prevention of typhoid and diphtheria have been held with an attendance each time of over 280."[6]

Later, in 1935, the annual report states, "Early in December of '34 we held our last clinic for the prevention of typhoid with 246 taking the treatment. With typhoid in various places about us, we did not have a single case."[7]

---

[2]Ruth Jenkins Muhlbauer, telephone interview by DruAnna W. Overbay, July 2002.

[3]Muhlbauer.

[4]Leonard. Vardy Community Presbyterian Church Records, 1932.

[5]Lloyd Williams, Vardy Oral Histories, interviewed by Katie Doman, Baltimore MD, 8 March 2000.

[6]Leonard, Vardy Community Presbyterian Church Records, 1934.

[7]Leonard, Vardy Community Presbyterian Church Records, 1934.

The popularity of the clinics was significant. People from other communities began to seek treatments there. Eventually the preacher divided his study into a front section to house the medical supplies that he had gotten to treat the people in the community. Miss Rankin, a nurse, had also accumulated several medical supplies that were stored in the mission house. Together they made a wonderful medical team.

While sharing stories about the clinic, Robert Moore said, "If we had colds, a sore throat, or anything, Preacher Leonard would swab our throats with iodine. Whenever anything was wrong, we stopped by the clinic on the way to school. It was located on the right as we walked up the steps to the school on the hill, right behind the Preacher's home."[8]

Genetically transmitted diseases such as lupus were untreatable by Reverend Leonard. However, he recognized the signs of disease when my sister Charlotte Williams, pictured here at age ten, returned from Warren Wilson High School for freshman-year Christmas break. The incurable disease claimed her life on Thanksgiving of her senior year.

Asked about the clinic, Muhlbauer told us, "Another thing that they did to ensure that we were healthy was to give us iodine pills, since our water did not have iodine in it. Miss Rankin was qualified to give us typhoid shots and the smallpox inoculation. If we got cut on the leg or something, Miss Rankin would clean it out and put a bandage on it. There was no other doctoring in Vardy other than the clinic."[9]

Lloyd Williams remarked, "Whenever we did have a bad wound, they would put some salve or something on it to keep it from getting infected, tape it up, and then keep a close watch on it. We would have to go by the

---

[8]Robert Moore, Vardy Oral Histories, interviewed by DruAnna Overbay, Talbott TN, 13 July 2002.

[9]Ruth Jenkins Muhlbauer, Vardy Oral Histories, interviewed by Katie Doman, Vardy Reunion, September 2000.

clinic for Mr. Leonard to look at it and put a new bandage on it every morning."[10]

Many of those interviewed were able to show the scars from their smallpox inoculations. Some claimed that as long as they lived they would be able to look at that scar and remember the day they got their shots. With those memories would come the feelings of love that they still had for Miss Rankin.

Deeply ingrained in the children was the fear of infectious diseases of the eyes. Since the trachoma problem during the late 1920s, everyone was concerned about anything getting into his eye. R. C. Mullins recalled, "If we got something in our eyes, we went immediately to the clinic. One day I got something in my eye, and Mr. Leonard used a syringe or an eyedropper to drop water in my eye to clean it, and then he dropped medicine in my eye to make sure it did not get infected. I remember being scared that I might go blind."[11]

"Preacher Leonard and Miss Rankin treated everybody so good," Audrey Mullins Franz said. "If we were sick, they would give us some pills to make us better. We would stand in line in the assembly room to get vitamins and cod liver oil to keep us healthy. We all took our medicine and didn't argue that we didn't want to take it. We trusted them to treat us and keep us healthy because they did everything for us."[12]

It seems to me that anytime anything happened to make me need a doctor, Mama sent me to Mr. Leonard's clinic. After going into the garden and eating unwashed raw vegetables, I had to be treated for roundworms. I went barefoot and had to be treated for hookworm. I can still remember how the medicine tasted. My mother would isolate me from my sisters and would not allow me to sleep in the same bed with them. She constantly scolded me for not wearing my shoes and for slipping into the garden.

When the itch was prevalent, she warned me not to hold hands with any of my friends. Needless to say, I got the itch. Preacher Leonard came to the rescue with a sulfur-based cream. This time I was isolated in the back room, where I had to rub the medicine all over me. Afterward, my mother burned all of my pajamas as well as the bed linens and washcloths that I had used.

---

[10]Lloyd Williams, Vardy Oral Histories..

[11]R. C. Mullins, Vardy Oral Histories, interviewed by DruAnna Overbay, Morristown TN, 15 June 2002.

[12]Audrey Mullins Franz, Vardy Oral Histories, interviewed by Katie Doman, Baltimore MD, March 2000.

None of my sisters or my brother ever had any of these problems. The only thing I never got was lice. When there was an infestation of lice in the community, Preacher Leonard checked our heads at the clinic before we were allowed to go to school. If a student were infested, he was sent home with specific instructions for treatment. He was not allowed to return until he was checked and found to be lice-free.

"Mr. Leonard's clinic was a big help to the community, and he had a good clinic. It was amazing how he got his training and supplies for it. The children would come for cod liver oil and other precautionary measures regarding colds and diet. It was a first aid stop. . . . He also kept health records on the students."[13]

Reverend Chester F. Leonard, shown here with sisters from a neighboring family, enjoyed being with children, who often asked him to play with them.

+ + + + +

Preacher Leonard's Game

There were no boundaries for me,
Preacher Leonard told me so
When Mama said, "You better quit
Slipping away from home, bothering him."

[13]David F. Swartz, Vardy Oral Histories, interviewed by DruAnna Overbay, Boone NC, 5 June 1999.

Past the crepe myrtle tree,
The pink rose bushes climbing the fence
Between Miss Rankin's and home
Pricked my skin until blood
Ran red

I was on a mission to sit on Preacher's lap
To hear the radio as he listened
For Joe Dimaggio's
Play

Blood dripping from my hands and arms,
I knocked on the screen.
"Come on in," he said
Carrying cotton balls and methiolate
He made a game of my wounds, I thought,
Swabbing the blood and marking
an "X" in the
Middle of each hand

"Remember this, my child,
Jesus died for our sins."

(A memory from childhood)

Chapter 9

Home Places

Scattered up and down the valley, on Newman's Ridge, and on Powell Mountain were the homes of the children who came to the school. Some came across the state line from Virginia because they all wanted to get the fine education the Presbyterians were offering. Their homes in the valley varied, depending upon the affluence of the families. Some interviewees were hesitant to describe their homes while others gave detailed descriptions.

Houses located in the hollow on Powell Mountain sat adjacent to the Vardy Community Presbyterian grounds at Horton's Corner. There Noah Collins and his brother-in-law, Dan Horton, had their homes.

During the late 1920s and early 1930s, Cleland and Oakey Collins lived with their Aunt Docia and Uncle Frank Miser. Cleland explained, "The house was T-shaped with four rooms: a kitchen/dining room combination, two bedrooms and a sitting/bedroom that had a fireplace where we sat during the winter. Each room had two windows. There were three porches—one on each side as well as the front, which had a southern exposure.

"There was a barn with stalls for the livestock and storage for hay and other feed. Also there was a shed to hang tobacco as well as a corn crib, a woodshed, a chicken house, and an outdoor toilet complete with the Sears and Roebuck catalogue."[1]

Horton's Corner was the crossroads for the roads up Vardy Valley and across Newman's Ridge and Powell Mountain. The Batey Collins home, on the right, also called the Long House, was located at the crossroads. In the center of the picture is Uncle Noah's store, which Papa Horton reopened after Noah's death. Back from boarding school in Asheville, Aunt Nelle Horton talks to her cousins who are inspecting Grandma Adelaide's washing that she had hung on the fence because the clotheslines were always full when Mama and her sisters came home for a visit.

My mom wrote in one of her manuscripts: "Our home in Vardy was a large three-room house. On one side were two large bedrooms. Each had two windows and an outside entrance. In the bedroom where my sisters and I slept were four beds (one for each of us), one dresser, two tables, and a chamber pot. We each had a drawer for our clothing in the dresser, and Nelle and I shared one table while Mossey and Isabelle shared the other. A large fireplace stood between the two bedrooms.

"There was a porch that went around the house, connecting to a detached kitchen and eating area. The chimney had a flue for the cookstove."[2]

Eula Mullins related, "We didn't even have a floor in our home. My mother was just as proud of that house as if it did. It was a log house and very cold in the winter, but we had all kinds of quilts that my mother had

[1]Cleland Collins, Vardy Oral Histories, interviewed by Sally Collins and DruAnna W. Overbay, Morristown TN, 25 April 1999.

[2]Alyce Horton Williams, "Remembering My Life," manuscript given to DruAnna Overbay.

made to put on our straw beds to keep us warm. She gave me some of her quilts when Loyal and I married. We moved off the ridge into the valley, on Drew Williams's place, where I was so proud to live because that house over by the Sulfur Springs was a plank house. Honey, when we moved in a plank house, it was like moving into a mansion."[3]

The last family who lived in the Mahala Mullins log cabin on Newman's Ridge was that of Laura and Hughie Mullins. Beulah Gibson and her brothers Leonard and Adam are visiting their cousin R. C. Mullins (right), who resided there until he was thirteen.

Born in a one-room log cabin in 1938, R. C. Mullins described his parents' and siblings' move in 1943: "I was almost five years old when we moved from there to the big Mahala Mullins house. We moved our things on a sled pulled by the horses. After our last load, we turned the animals loose, and they just followed us out the ridge as if they knew we were moving.

"We only used the first large room of the cabin. It was our living room and bedroom. We had three beds and homemade chairs that we used to sit around the fireplace. My mother and dad slept in one bed; my two brothers and I slept in one; and my sister slept in the other.

"Now, the dog-trot was closed off when I lived there. Planks had been nailed to either end to make a kitchen. It had a large wooden table with six legs, wooden dynamite boxes to sit on, a cook stove on one side of it, a smaller table that had water buckets and a washbasin to wash our hands and faces.

---

[3]Eula Mullins, Vardy Oral Histories, interviewed by Katie Doman, Baltimore MD, March 2000.

"The next large room was so badly deteriorated that we just used it for junk. We never built a fire in that fireplace. We didn't use the upstairs except to hang tobacco up there. After Ralph got older, we cleaned that room up for his bedroom. I remember seeing snow on his bed during the winter. It would just come down the stairs because the cracks between the logs hadn't been chinked in a long time.

"Looking back, I don't know how we lived. We could have frozen there, but we survived. I have seen water freeze in the living room in that cabin. During winter wash days, Mother would bring a tub of water to warm at the foot of our bed. It often didn't. One day it froze so hard that we could stand on it. Having no electricity in that house, we had to study after dark by lamplight. Sometimes we would lie in front of the fireplace and read. Of course, there wasn't a bathroom."[4]

This house was occupied by several different families, including the Sizemores, the Misers, the Jayneses, and the Mullinses.

Describing his home, Charles Sizemore said, "I lived in three different houses that were fairly good for an average house in the valley. Our first house had a fireplace, but wood stoves heated the other two. We didn't have electricity in the first two, but at the first house, where I was born, my dad had a Delco generator for lights in the house and the store. In one there was an upstairs that was too cold for sleeping in the winter. On our beds we had springs, mattresses, and a feather tick on each. But some people didn't . . . they had straw ticks on rope beds.

"There was a barn to house livestock as well as hang tobacco. We put the hay in the barn during late winter after the tobacco went to market.

---

[4]R. C. Mullins, Vardy Oral Histories, interviewed by DruAnna Overbay, Morristown TN, 15 June 2002.

When the hay was cut, it was stacked in the fields to be hauled to the barn as needed on a horse-drawn wagon."[5]

"Many people lived in two-room houses that belonged to other people," said Lloyd Williams. "These families would tend to the crops and were called renters. They didn't have to pay to live there, but they did have to work the fields. We owned our own home in the valley. It was basically a square house: two rooms in the front, two rooms in the back. Over time we added to it and stretched it out to a six-room rectangle. We had a living room, a kitchen, dining room, two bedrooms, and a front porch as well as a back porch.

Helping finish family chores are Troy, Lloyd, and Mae, with their mother Little Williams.

"The boys had to sleep together, three to a bed. Then my sisters slept in the same bed. My parents slept in the other bedroom. We didn't have a mattress until we got to be teenagers. We slept on a straw bed with a quilt on top of it to keep it from being so rough. We had wood heat, but the fire would go out and the house would get very cold, but we had enough quilts over our beds to stay warm. Also we had a featherbed, which was the most important part. It was fluffy and really felt good because it was so thick."[6]

Remembering the warmth from featherbeds, Audrey Mullins Franz believed it to be a common experience of most in the valley. "We didn't have mattresses, but straw ticks. It was a tick sewn on both sides that straw was stuffed in and then sewn at the top. We would just put a plain sheet

---

[5]Charles Sizemore, Vardy Oral Histories, interviewed by Katie Dorman, Vardy Church, Sneedville TN, February 2000.

[6]Lloyd Williams, Vardy Oral Histories, interviewed by Katie Doman, Baltimore MD, 8 March 2000.

over that, and then quilts and a featherbed. Straw was on the bottom and feathers on the top. It was almost impossible to make. We had to keep the beds looking smooth because Mom's beds had to be straight and perfect. With the featherbed, quilts, and blankets, the only things that would get cold were our noses, and sometimes they would feel like icicles."[7]

Lloyd Sizemore was born in this house on Newman's Ridge, which is also where his grandparents had their homeplace. Julie Stewart is standing on the left, Elizabeth Goins Sizemore (Lloyd's mother) is seated in a chair at the front of the porch. Lloyd is seated on the porch.

"Many of the houses when I was younger were very much like the Pennsylvania Dutch. Clay Miser's house was a large two-story house with beautiful carving similar to gingerbread carvings on both the upper- and lower-level porches. These were the homes that I remember, but the houses in the valley were changed greatly when the tornado came in 1933. The homes of Harrison Collins and Grant Collins were badly damaged. Much smaller ones replaced both. Andy Gibson's home was badly damaged, but not enough for replacement. It finally burned," my mama wrote.[8]

"Our mother and dad lived in Great-Grandpa Batey's house during the first years of their marriage," recalled my brother Dan. "My mom was pregnant with me when the tornado hit, but she got under the bed for protection. The storm did damage the home, but we were safe. I was born in that house, but we did not continue living there. The damage was so bad

---

[7]Audrey Mullins Franz, Vardy Oral Histories, interviewed by Katie Doman, Baltimore MD, March 2000.

[8]Alyce Horton Williams, "Remembering My Life," manuscript given to DruAnna Overbay.

that they decided to build a new house behind that old log cabin. That house still stands today."[9]

In the annual reports, Chester F. Leonard recorded that "On the night of March 14, the great wind storm blew down our houses, barns, and sheds, uprooted trees and tore down fences, killing two of the people of our community, Lily Sexton and Emmett Moore. For about a day we sat back rather stunned, and then we went to work. Today our houses and barns, for the most part, are back in better condition than before the storms. With a little push and boost, the loan of different things, the replacement of dishes, etc., we again were ready to go. The school was damaged some; Miss Rankin's house had to be entirely replaced; and other damage to our property added to the difficulties caused by the closing of the banks."[10]

During the 1930s my parents built their new house in the same location as the houses of Horton Corners. Their garage, which was to the left of the ivy-covered rock wall occupies the same space as did Grandpa Batey and Cynthia Collins's long house.

When I was born to Drew and Alyce Williams, their new house had electricity, but oil lamps were kept ready for frequent power outages. One entered the house by going up concrete steps, onto a porch which wrapped around the living and dining room. The front door took one into the living room. On the left was my parents' bedroom. Through the living room's double doors was the dining room, and to the left my sisters and I shared the middle bedroom. A short hall to the bathroom from the dining room also went to my brother's room. The kitchen was behind the dining room. It had a door on the left that went to a back porch and the attached smokehouse. There was a flue in each room except the front bedroom and

9Daniel H. Williams, Vardy Oral Histories, interviewed by DruAnna Overbay, Knoxville TN, 15 June 2002.

10Chester F. Leonard, "Annual Reports," Vardy Community Presbyterian Church Records, 1933.

dining room. I do not remember any stoves except the one in the living room and the old cookstove in the kitchen. Below the house was the cellar, which had both an outside entrance and a downstairs entrance between the two back bedrooms. Each room had two or more large windows. The house of lapped siding was built on a solid rock foundation.

One of the many cabins located on Newman's Ridge overlooking the Vardy Valley when the Rev. Chester F. Leonard came to the Vardy Community. Powell Mountain is in the background.

Robert Moore remarked, "We lived in a log cabin that had a fireplace. There were two large rooms. We had three beds in one room where the kids slept. In the other room, my mom and dad slept. It had a bed, a little cookstove, our table, and chairs. It was a bedroom, a kitchen, and living room in one. Eventually, my dad built a little room on the back for a kitchen. Then he built a long table with benches on each side. As the kids kept coming, he cut a hole to the loft for stairs for the boys to have a place to sleep. He put a window in both ends. It was so cold that we slept with our heads under the covers. I recall pushing the covers back and finding snow on us.

"The house was papered with newspaper. We mixed flour and water to make glue to hold the paper onto the planks. We put the paper over and over until it was about an inch thick. It would pull away from the boards. Another incident that I remember is that a snake had crawled between the boards and the paper."[11]

---

[11]Robert Moore, Vardy Oral Histories, interviewed by DruAnna Overbay, Talbott TN, 13 July 2002.

In 1928 my mother,
Alyce Horton (Williams),
began college at
Lincoln Memorial University,
where she met my father.

+ + + + +

A Daughter's Guilt
Reflections of Mama
Alyce Williams
1909–1991

Mama,
You
Were only twenty-two
When your mother died
And I?
I was only forty-nine.

You
Spoke of your grief
At her dying.
Was it deeper than mine?

You grieved for sixty years,
Compared to my
Sixty days
Of unsurfacing tears.

Yet,
A month before
You left me,
You said,
"I wish you
had known my mother."

Well,
Now that you're gone
I wish I had known mine,
But I
Never took the time
To listen,
To know,
To learn,
All you had to teach.

Chapter 10

Livelihood

Of living on top of Newman's Ridge with his mother Atcie Collins, three sisters, and four brothers, W. C. Collins remembered, "We had a little ridge farm where we worked, growing corn and tobacco and gardening. We had cows for milk, hogs for meat, chickens for eggs, and a team of horses for farming and transportation."[1]

Most of those interviewed spoke of the gardens that the families maintained. Charles Sizemore said, "My mother raised a huge garden. She canned everything. She had hundreds and hundreds of cans of vegetables and fruits. We butchered hogs, and what wasn't stored in the smokehouse my mother would can, like the ribs and sausage."[2]

Dad was proud of this hog, which my brother Dan had fattened for butchering. County agent at the time Fred Zachary examines the hogs to enter in 4-H contests.

Relating how her mother Nancy Collins Miser sent the children to get apples to make fried-apple turnovers and stack cakes, Claribel Miser Horton declared, "My mother was an excellent cook. Nobody ever came to visit that she would not send one of us out in the yard to wring a chicken's neck so that she could fry it for company. We made apple butter and pear butter and picked berries for cobblers. One of our favorite activities was gathering nuts—chinquapins, hickory nuts, and walnuts. She used every-

[1]W. C. Collins, Vardy Oral Histories, interviewed by Katie Doman, Sneedville TN, 7 August 2000.

[2]Charles Sizemore, Vardy Oral Histories, interviewed by Katie Dorman, Vardy Church, Sneedville TN, February 2000.

thing to make her desserts. She made a sweet cake that we called a lard cake. She ran a fork across the dough to make a cross and spread it with beaten eggs.

"My father raised all of our meat. We butchered cattle, hogs, and chickens and raised all of the food that we canned. We had a large family so it took all of us girls working in the garden. The boys would help Dad on the farm with the corn, tobacco, and hay. We milked our cows and gathered the eggs."[3]

Haying on the Lloyd Sizemore farm includes Lloyd on the rake and Clay Sexton on the mule. Left of the rake are Bradley Collins, Hubert Bell, Noah Bell, and Albert Mullins.

Audrey Mullins Franz continued, "Everything that we ate, such as cabbages, onions, potatoes, beans, carrots, beets, turnips, corn, lettuce, tomatoes, we grew . . . we grew everything in the garden."

Even though I remember eating many of the spring greens, I do not know how to identify them. My brother Dan has promised to show me the different kinds. He told me, "In the spring I would help my mother pick greens to cook. Among those that we gathered were mouse's ear, blue stem, dandelions, wild mustard, round leaf plantain, and lamb's quarters. Lamb's quarters was cooked by itself because it had such a mellow flavor. It tastes like spinach. My mother was always a little bit afraid of poke, and so we didn't have poke salad very often. Sometimes she would peel the stalk, slice it length-wise, roll it in meal, and fry it. It was good that way. Other

---

[3]Claribel Miser Horton, Vardy Oral Histories, interviewed by DruAnna W. Overbay, Seymour IN, 17 July 1999.

times she would parboil the poke leaves and then fry them. If we wanted to be just a little bit naughty, we would slip some elderberry shoots into the greens. That would send those who ate the salad to the outhouse in a hurry."[4]

Oakey Collins told me, "Of course, we didn't have refrigerators and freezers back then, so some of the food would be dried, some of it would be canned, and then some of it would be buried in the ground. We would dig large holes to put our apples, potatoes, and cabbage in and cover them up with straw and dirt so the vegetables would not freeze during the winter."[5]

Our cellar was filled every summer with the bounties of Mama's garden. She carefully inspected every jar left from the previous year to determine if she should dispose of its contents. Helping her with this task were my sisters Margaret and Charlotte Williams.

And Audrey Mullins Franz related that "We preserved everything in jars. We didn't have a refrigerator. We had a dairy dug in the ground in the side of the ridge, where Mom kept all of her canned food. She would can string beans, corn, and everything she could. She would also pickle corn, beets, and cucumbers. Now, potatoes, we dug a big hole in the ground, made a big straw bed, put the potatoes in it, covered it over with more straw, and then covered that with a lot of dirt. She had a little hole where she would dig her potatoes out. They would stay in that hole all winter."[6]

[4]Daniel H. Williams, Vardy Oral Histories.

[5]Oakey Hendrix Collins, Vardy Oral Histories, interviewed by DruAnna Overbay, Morristown TN, 25 August 1999.

[6]Audrey Mullins Franz, Vardy Oral Histories, interviewed by Katie Doman, Baltimore MD, March 2000.

Franz described the in-ground storage facility as a round hole about three to five feet in depth. The straw was sufficient to keep the vegetables from freezing.

Lloyd Williams confirmed, "We had to go deep—let's say about thirty inches or more, put straw in the bottom, then apples, turnips, carrots, everything we wanted to keep, and put more straw on. Each layer of straw was three or four inches deep. Then we would put a big mound of dirt over that.

"Some underground cellars had a shed over the top of them, and some were just covered up with logs about 8 to 12 inches in diameter and then covered. There were doors to the cellars which were also used as protection from storms and high winds, so they served two purposes. . . . We kept potatoes in a big wooden box in the cellar since the potatoes had to be stored separately from the apples because the potatoes would cause the apples to spoil right away. The apples were stored in a hole by themselves."[7]

A drummer (traveling salesman) came down the road and picked up the chickens and eggs that had been bartered at the store. Because the road to Vardy was poorly maintained, he often became stuck in the mud.

Troy Williams recalled that "People in our community were survivors and had many survival skills. They were able to make do with what they had and learned to barter early. We had a bartering system that allowed those who lived in the valley to trade with those who lived on Powell Mountain or Newman's Ridge. . . . We grew Irish potatoes, sweet potatoes, and other root vegetables in the valley that were hard to grow on the mountain and ridge because of how rocky it was. Up at the homes of R. C. Mullins and Robert Moore, they had wonderful fruit trees so we would barter vegetables and fruit. We would take eggs to Bill Grohse's store and exchange them for salt, sugar, and other staples. Earlier our families would

---

[7]Lloyd Williams, Vardy Oral Histories, interviewed by Katie Doman, Baltimore MD, 8 March 2000.

take corn and wheat to the mills to be ground, and the mill owners would take a portion for their work."[8]

Ralph Mullins, shown here with a working mule, John, helped farmers in the area by plowing their fields.

Lewis A. Williams wrote, "When my grandmother Rosa Bell Alder set one of her bountiful country meals no one went hungry. There was always freshly baked cornbread. She would also serve green beans, either fresh or from her stock of canned goods. Fresh tomatoes and green peppers in season, okra, potatoes, and meat or fish were served.

"The meat varied from beef, chicken, or pork, to wild game—rabbit, squirrel, or groundhog. Rosa ate squirrel brains, considering it the best part of those bushy critters! The fish were caught by Grandpa Lewis from the Blackwater Creek or the Clinch River and included catfish, suckers, carp, brim, and bass. Occasionally, they had turtle.

"Desserts ranged from large sugar cookies, vanilla or chocolate cake with boiled frosting, blueberry, blackberry, peach or apple pies. When eggs were plentiful, she would make egg custard pie! No one ever went hungry. Life was busy and the work was hard; most families had limited material possessions, but they led happy and rewarding lives."[9]

Even though there was electricity in the valley during the late 1940s, Dave Swartz recalled that when he was a seminary intern living in the Rankin House on the Presbyterian grounds, "There was not a refrigerator in the Rankin House, so I would place my milk into a pan of cool water and

---

[8]Troy Williams, personal comments to DruAnna Overbay, 1996–2002.

[9]Lewis A. Williams, "Rosa Bell Alder—A Foundation Stone of the Vardy Community," Vardy Memory Book, submitted to DruAnna Overbay, 22 November 2002.

put that in the little cellar dug into the hill area right behind the rear porch. Things would stay reasonably cool in there, but after a day or so the milk would curdle."[10]

Few people had refrigerators in the early 1940s. Lloyd Williams said, "We had spring houses to keep milk, butter, and leftover food cool. . . . Our spring house had a concrete bottom in it. A trench ran to it, which carried the water through it so that six or eight inches of water ran from the spring. We would set our food in there so it kept cool. The trench then ran to the ditch in the back where the water went on to the creek. The water was very cool. It was the only way to keep our milk from spoiling."[11]

Rosa Delp is shown with her grandsons, cutting tobacco on the Drew Williams farm during the 1950s.

Geraldine Hatfield Bell remembered that "Getting electricity in our home was unforgettable because my dad [Lonnie Hatfield] bought a refrigerator for Mom to store the milk. Drinking milk cooled in the refrigerator took me a while to get used to because it was so cold it hurt my teeth. We had been used to milk cooled in the spring house."[12]

Franz, who carried water from the spring, which flowed out of the ridge, said, "The spring came out of the rocks in the ridge. We would put our buckets under the rocks and fill them. A hole had been dug there to catch the water, but Mom would not allow us to fill our buckets from the hole. We got our water as it came out of the rocks. There was a pond below

---

[10]David F. Swartz, Vardy Oral Histories, interviewed by DruAnna Overbay, Boone NC, 5 June 1999.

[11]Lloyd Williams, Vardy Oral Histories.

[12]Geraldine Hatfield Bell, Vardy Oral Histories, interviewed by DruAnna W. Overbay, Blountville TN, 19 August 1999.

the spring that the excess water ran into where we would bring the horses to let them drink."

When questioned about the water's being sulfur water, Franz replied, "No, it was limestone water . . . water coming from Sulfur Springs smells like rotten eggs."[13]

Boyd Ward Collins wrote, "The families in Vardy were industrious despite and perhaps because of their remoteness. All of our forebears were very hardworking, and we were taught from the earliest age that if we worked hard, saved, etc., that we would succeed." They managed to provide for their families by selling corn, tobacco, and livestock and by logging.[14]

During the 1910s, stacks of straw made good bed ticks. These stacks were on my grandparents' (Dan and Adelaide Horton) farm, inherited from her father Batey Collins. My mom inherited the farm from Adelaide; thus for generations the original Vardemon Collins farm has been in direct descendant ownership.

In more recent times, they provided the field rock for many buildings in East Tennessee. One Vardy school alumnus sold rocks for Dolly Parton's home in Sevierville, buildings at Dollywood, various banks of Knoxville, Morristown, and Kingsport, as well as civic buildings and other private homes. Clarence Williams, one of the most industrious and financially successful of the rock suppliers in East Tennessee, stated, "I supplied rock to seven different states, including Maryland, Pennsylvania, West Virginia, Virginia, South Carolina, North Carolina, and Georgia."[15]

Because money was scarce, many gathered walnuts and bartered them for food staples such as sugar, salt, flour, or meal. Others owned the mills that ground the wheat and corn. Store owners and operators could be found up and down the valley during the early part of the twentieth century. Lloyd Sizemore owned a store that he later sold to Bill Grohse.[16] Prior to those

[13] Audrey Franz, Vardy Oral Histories.

[14] Boyd Ward Collins, personal correspondence to DruAnna W. Overbay, 18 August 1981.

[15] Clarence Williams, personal comments to DruAnna Overbay, October 1999.

[16] Charles Sizemore, Vardy Oral Histories.

stores, my grandfather, whom we called Papa Horton, owned a store, not only in Vardy but also in Mulberry.

Lloyd Williams informed us, "My dad Ed Williams worked for the Hancock County Road Department in road maintenance. Most families had small tobacco allotments where they grew tobacco. Selling the tobacco would bring in $150 or $200 a year. . . . When we got to be teenagers, we began helping out a little more. My brother Ott [Austin] and I did a lot of logging for mining timbers and pulpwood. That would bring in $60 or $80 a week, which was a chunk of money at that time. . . . We went into the woods with a crosscut saw, just a piece of steel with teeth in it, and we would yank it back and forth. In later years we bought a powersaw, a chainsaw. . . . We brought the logs off the mountain and ridge by a mule pulling them down. . . . I'd say that we pulled them down three-fourths of a mile or longer."[17]

Logan and Nancy Miser's young children are shown riding Maude, their horse, in the 1920s. Led by Ernest Miser are Florence Marie, Gladys, Claribel, and Walter.

Robert Moore remembered that "The people I knew were mostly farmers. My dad farmed for other people and cut some mining props. He worked for the road department some and in the mines in Bonnie Blue, Virginia. I can remember him being gone from time to time. He talked about working for fifty cents a day and later a dollar a day. I know that when I was probably about twelve or fourteen, I was working for a dollar a day cutting corn, tobacco, and bushes. Most of the people made a living on the farms. That was about all the work in that vicinity. . . .

[17]Lloyd Williams, Vardy Oral Histories.

"Where we lived it was hard to raise livestock. When I was eight or nine years old, we owned some mountain land and had a few cattle, but it seemed they were about as poor as we were because we were having a hard time making a living. The ground was so rough and rocky and stayed grown up in weeds. We had a team of mules that we tried to work the ground with. We never really went hungry, but we didn't have any luxuries.

"We raised hogs and chickens as well as most of the food we ate. . . . My mother and dad had so many children. . . . They had to have quite a bit of food on that table to feed all of those children. We were lucky in that where we lived we had a lot of apple, pear and cherry trees. And, of course, I helped pick blackberries for fifteen cents a gallon. I made most of my money for clothing by digging May apple roots and cracking walnuts. . . . There was no money, as far as allowance. I didn't know what that was when I was a kid."[18]

A pen-and-ink drawing by artist Don Britton of Aunt Mahala in front of her log cabin.

Dan Williams recalled, "Digging herbs was one of the ways that I earned spending money. I dug May apple roots, snake roots, yellow dock roots, and ginseng and sold them. . . . In addition to that, I trapped muskrats. I would stretch their pelts over a board to dry. Afterward, I would send the furs off to Sears. The pelts would usually bring around a dollar or two. I will never forget that I had what I thought was the prettiest fur and felt sure that I would get five dollars for it. When I got the statement back from Sears, it brought only fifty cents because it was a 'kit' (a baby muskrat). . . . One time I found a red fox dead in the road. I skinned it and dried it. That

---

[18]Robert Moore, Vardy Oral Histories, interviewed by DruAnna Overbay, Talbott TN, 13 July 2002.

was the worst smelling animal I ever fooled with. Anyway, I sold that to Sears, too. It did bring five dollars."[19]

Previous to that time, fur traders came into the valley to buy furs from the early settlers. To provide these early traders a place to stay, several cabins were built around the sulfur springs. During the Civil War, all were burned by the Rebels but one. The men in the valley had gone to fight for the Yankees. The one cabin left standing was named for Vardemon Collins. Known as the Vardy Springs Hotel, it sat on the main road, at that time, through Vardy near Sulfur Springs and was the crossroads for a road going over Newman's Ridge and continuing up the valley. Later, when the road changed and no longer crossed over Blackwater Creek, my great-grandfather, Batey Collins, moved and opened his home to boarders, which became known as the Collins Boarding House. Because of a drastic decrease in the fur trade and with the road change, there were fewer guests in the hotel, which continued to operate until Batey's death. Mom told me that her father tore down the hotel, took the timbers to Ewing, Virginia, and built a home there across from the old Lee County Industrial High School, where she, her sisters, and cousins attended school. When I visited Cecil Hoskins, a member of the Hancock County Historical Society who lives in Ewing, we drove by the house that my Papa Horton built from those timbers. The house is still standing and has been well maintained.

A close friendship between cousins Alyce Horton Williams and Helen Stewart Mullins was enjoyed for many years as they shared teaching roles at the Vardy Community church and school.

---

[19]Daniel H. Williams, Vardy Oral Histories, interviewed by DruAnna Overbay, Knoxville TN, 15 June 2002.

There are, of course, as with any remote mountainous area, tales of moonshining. However, few of those interviewed mentioned moonshining. They did have in mind people who were part of the business but declined to give any specific information or to name anyone. In Jim Callahan's article "The First Missionaries in Blackwater," printed in the May 2002 issue of *Vardy Voice*, he quotes one of the early Presbyterian missionaries Margaret McCall: "[Some members of the community] made moonshine whiskey and had 'blind tigers' (places where intoxicants were illegally sold on the sly)."[20]

Moore, however, did tell about his father's moonshining: "Everybody knew that my dad was a moonshiner. There just wasn't any other way for him to be able to make a living because there were so many in our family. I remember him sending me to the bootlegger's with two burlap sacks of moonshine. He put corn shucks around the jars to keep them from breaking and to make it look like we were transporting corn. One time I met the sheriff and his deputy on their way to our house. Dad had just made a run of moonshine and had loaded the mule with my two sacks. He had hidden the rest of it in the cellar under the smokehouse. My heart was racing so fast that I thought it would jump out of my chest. I felt sure that I would be caught and Dad would go to jail. The sheriff talked to me a long time while I sat on that mule waiting for him to search the bags. He never did ask me what I had in the bags. I thought he would watch to see if I would go to the bootlegger's, but I turned my mule down the road toward Vardy and didn't take it directly to the bootlegger's."[21]

Other stories abound about moonshiners, one of whom was Mahala Collins Mullins. Much has been written about her, and it is difficult to tell what is truth and what has been fictionalized. Sensationalism always sells, often at the expense of destroying reputations. The VCHS moved Mahala's cabin off Newman's Ridge after it was donated by Daniel H. Williams, the last owner of the cabin, so that it can be more easily maintained and visited.

Boyd Ward Collins wrote, "One of the ambitions of my life is to walk up to my grandmother's old cabin someday. I have only seen it from the Vardy Road and understand it is quite a hike. Martha Collins wrote in a letter to me, 'Wouldn't it be wonderful if the cabin could be restored.' She said that it had been a lovely large two-story structure with a dog trot

---

[20]Jim Callahan, "The First Missionaries in Blackwater," *Vardy Voice*, May 2002.

[21]Moore, Vardy Oral Histories.

between the two major rooms, and what was often thought to be the cabin was nothing more than a crib, shed, barn, or some other outer structure."[22]

Aunt Mahala's many great-grandchildren and other relatives are involved in the historical endeavor at Vardy. Those who have been able to visit the relocated and restored cabin have voiced their happiness that VCHS has made it possible for them to see it. Boyd Collins, however, has not been able to do so even though his brothers Cleland and Oakey spent many hours there during the MHA gathering in June 2001.

R. C. Mullins told me, "Mahala's land, which Dan's parents bought from my parents, Laura and Hughie Mullins, had many other owners. Aunt Mahala may have inherited it from her parents Solomon D. Collins and Jincie Goins, early settlers in Vardy."[23] Some speculate that her husband John Mullins may have inherited it from his father, known as Irish Jim.

That farm as well as the adjacent ones was always a favored hunting area. Some of those interviewed remembered hunting rabbits, squirrels, and opossums for food. "We had opossum and sweet potatoes sometimes to eat, and it was really good. Mom would fry rabbits and squirrels and also make rabbit stew and squirrel dumplings. We knew how to eat and use everything. It was called survival."[24]

Charles Sizemore laughingly recalled, "Most of the hunting I did was at night. I wasn't ever allowed to have a gun to go hunting with when I was real young. We would just hunt opossum . . . catch them."[25]

Another form of livelihood in the community was teaching. Both of my parents and Helen Mullins were teachers in the Vardy Community as well as farmers. Eula Mullins Collins and her husband were sharecroppers on the Williams farm. Eula also took in ironing from the Williams and Grohse families.

Other means of providing for families involved quilting and woodwork. "One of the times that I was with my mother during a quilting session," Dan Williams remembered, "some of the women were talking about a young lady in the community who was developing quite a reputation. One of the women asked Mother Grohse (Bill's German step-mother who had moved here from New York) what she thought about the girl. In her broken

---

[22]Boyd Collins, personal letters.

[23]R. C. Mullins, Vardy Oral Histories, interviewed by DruAnna Overbay, Talbott TN, 15 June 2002.

[24]R. C. Mullins, Vardy Oral Histories.

[25]Sizemore, Vardy Oral Histories.

English and German accent, she replied, 'I saz nutin'. I seez nutin'. I don't a-talk about nosbody.' For a youngster hearing that, I thought that was a pretty good lesson to learn."[26]

During earlier times community residents made baskets and chairs as well as caned chair bottoms. One of those was Alex Stewart, who lived on Newman's Ridge. Alex became well known during his later years and was featured in John Rice Irwin's Museum of Appalachia. Stewart was the subject of many of Irwin's writings. His grandson carries on the tradition of basket making by utilizing some of the same methods as his grandfather, such as soaking white oak strips to make the wood more pliable and to form various shapes.

The Vardy Church Museum recently received an egg basket from Louise Avery, the last missionary to have lived in Vardy. Mrs. Leonard had given her the egg basket, which was perhaps made by Lewis Johnson. Ruth Muhlbauer tells me that she too has one of the egg baskets from Mrs. Leonard. According to Ruth, Lewis Johnson made those baskets and gave them as gifts. Lewis was very active in the church and community when Ruth was a child.

While they were growing up in the valley, those interviewed remembered that George Johnson made outdoor furniture out of vines and twigs, leaving the twigs exposed for a more rustic look. He usually made a double chair, a single chair, a rocker, and both tall and short tables. His furniture looked much like wicker.

The Community Store

Since money was scarce, groceries were often charged by the storeowners' patrons. Early storeowners included Daniel B. Horton. During part of 1905–1915 and during the 1920s, his brother-in-law Noah Collins owned and operated that store. Some other storeowners were Howard Collins, Monleys Collins, Burkett Mullins, Lloyd Sizemore, Albert Mullins, and Bill Grohse. Early storeowners accepted wheat or corn as payment, since they also had mills, which ground the wheat into flour or the corn into meal.

"When I was a youngster living with Asa Gibson and his sons Gilbert and Coby Gibson in the Aunt Mahala log cabin," Roland Collins remembered, "I would bring sacks of corn off the ridge to grind at the mill that

---

[26]Daniel H. Williams, Vardy Oral Histories.

had been Daniel Boone Horton's mill at Vardy in the Horton's Corner across the road from Alyce and Drew's home. Daniel Horton also had a store there that my father Crodell Collins used to work in when he was young."[27]

Docia Collins Miser took over her father's mill when he died. When local farmers brought grain to the mill, they paid a toll for having it ground. The toll box measured the amount of grain that was paid for that service.

Most of those interviewed who were in their sixties remembered when Bill Grohse was the storeowner. "If we had a grocery bill or owed something for $80 that year, we'd pay it off with the tobacco crop," recalled Lloyd Williams.[28] Lloyd's brother Troy added, "One time our family owed the entire earnings from the tobacco crop to Bill Grohse because we had charged that much in groceries."[29]

Evidently, operating a store became a chosen profession for the Sizemore family. After the death of Charles Sizemore's father, his mother operated a store on the Tennessee-Virginia state line on the other side of Powell Mountain from Vardy. Today their son Charles owns and operates the Outpost Trading Post four miles east of Jonesville, Virginia.

To supplement the tobacco income, many families raised livestock. Lloyd Williams continued, "A lot of people had a lot of cattle . . . we thought thirty head of cattle was a big cattle farm back then. They'd raise calves from the cattle and sell them for thirty-five or forty dollars to have money. Some people would raise hogs. Not a whole lot of them . . . maybe twenty-five. That was a lot of hogs to a poor person. They would sell those

---

[27]Roland Collins, personal comments to DruAnna Overbay, Vardy School Reunion, Fall 2002.

[28]Lloyd Williams, Vardy Oral Histories.

[29]Troy Williams, personal comments to author.

for five or six dollars—the small ones. Maybe the larger ones they would either keep or sell them for sixteen, eighteen, or twenty dollars."[30]

Dan recalled that "Everybody up and down the valley cracked walnuts and took the kernels to Bill Grohse's store to sell or trade for whatever we needed. . . . I think one of the happiest days of my life was when eggs went to twelve cents a dozen because that meant that I wouldn't have to take two eggs to get a penny's worth of candy. . . . Of course, we did little chores around the house, and our mother gave us eggs that we could take to the store and trade for candy, cookies, or gum. Bill was always a nice man who would give us candy when we came into the store for our parents. Lillian and Bill were always good to us when we were children. Aunt Nancy, my mother's aunt and Lillian's mother, was too. There were just a lot of good-hearted people who lived around there."[31]

Fresh produce was sold by William Gibson, who went to South Carolina to purchase watermellons and peaches for Vardy residents.

Troy Williams remembered, "Drew and Alyce had a lot of chickens that would lay their eggs sometimes on the side of the road in those orange tiger lilies or the sweet peas. If they didn't lay in the henhouse, we felt it was okay to get those eggs and take them to the store."[32]

Charles Sizemore laughed about taking the eggs also, and he remembered how he bartered them: "When you're young, I guess you think that

---

[30]Lloyd Williams, Vardy Oral Histories.
[31]Daniel H. Williams, Vardy Oral Histories.
[32]Troy Williams, Vardy Oral Histories.

you'd like to smoke. I remember getting into Drew Williams's hen nest on the side of the road and taking enough eggs to get a bag of Old Horse Stacks Smoking Tobacco. The first cigarette I ever had was rolled out of some of that tobacco."[33]

Store owner Bill Grohse, in overalls, entertains ministerial intern Dave Swartz with stories about Lowell Collins's and Nina Delph's ancestors.

During the summer months, people were able to sell fruits and berries. Lloyd Williams observed that "Right up next to the top of the mountain were fruit trees like cherries, apples, pears, and peaches. They would bring down the fruit for the people in the valley, who could get a gallon of cherries for something like fifty or seventy-five cents . . . we'd get fruit by the sackfuls, burlap bags full. . . . Fifty cents for all that we could carry of apples. I used to go with my mother and get a lot of those. . . . We picked berries. Called them huckleberries, not blueberries. . . . And we'd pick blackberries. . . . We sold berries. . . . We're talking about twenty-five gallons at a time, thirty. We would take them into Virginia and come back with sixteen or eighteen dollars, which was a lot of money. And that was a big help to us.

"My mother did gather a lot of walnuts. . . . She'd carry them two miles . . . from an old farm over there. The guy's name was Johnny McDaniel . . . and we'd go over there and take all the green hulls off them and hide them in the woods . . . then, we'd go back later and bring them all home . . . my mother would spread them all out behind the stove. Not all we had, just

---

[33]Sizemore, Vardy Oral Histories.

whatever she was going to crack out that day . . . and the kernels, she would let dry behind the wood stove. Then she would work with those for three or four hours each night to get three or four dollars."[34]

Families who lived on Newman's Ridge often brought a mule and sled down to carry home their grocery staples such as salt, sugar, flour, and other groceries. Here Laura Mullins and her children Betty and RC a.re on the way to Grohse's store.

Outmigration

As in many Appalachian communities, outmigration took residents to other states. Some stayed as close as Kentucky by going into the coalfields in Harlan, Benham, and Lynch during 1910–1925, eventually making their homes there and in the Big Stone Gap area, just across the mountain from Lynch. Prior to the Presbyterians' arrival in 1897, church records indicate that a number of families migrated up into Pike County, Kentucky. During the late 1920s, 1930s, and early 1940s, many of the Bales, Collins, and Horton families went into southern Indiana to the farmlands and canning factories. The Miser families followed older siblings into Indiana and farther north into Illinois, where Grace Miser Taylor had moved after her husband became one of the Presbyterian ministers in Rockwood. Many of the Mullins families moved to Ohio and the northern part of Indiana after World War II and during the 1950s. Collins, Jenkins, Mullins, Goins, and Williams families moved into the Baltimore, Maryland, area during that time frame. Making a living as a sharecropper or storekeeper, farming, or just plain living off the land became less of an option as children who had been educated at Vardy Community School envisioned more prosperous livelihoods.

---

[34]Lloyd Williams, Vardy Oral Histories.

Step-grandmother Claribel Horton (back row center) would take us to visit with her mother, Great-Aunt Nancy Miser (top row, second from left). Others on the back row are Clabibel's sisters. On the front row are Vardy Collins, Claribel's daughter Lorene Horton (our aunt), my sisters Charlotte and Margaret Williams,and Claribel's son Daniel Boone Horton, Jr. (our uncle).

A family photograph of Aunt Nancy and all of her children who came home for a family reunion.

Katie Doman wrote, "Although they all consider Vardy their 'home,' many of the people I interviewed left the valley shortly after finishing their last year at Vardy Community School. Some of them went to Presbyterian-run high schools in North Carolina: The Asheville Farm School for Boys and Dorland-Bell for the girls, which later combined to become Warren Wilson High School and College, a Presbyterian college in Swannanoa, North Carolina. A number of students graduated from Presbyterian-affiliated colleges."[35]

One of those who was educated at the Dorland-Bell School for Girls in Hot Springs, North Carolina, was Ruth Jenkins Muhlbauer, who remembered: "I was very homesick away from home, but it wasn't as lonely as I would have been if Gwendolyn Delph hadn't been there with me. When I

---

[35]Katie Doman, submitted manuscript to *Windows on the Past*, 20 June 2002.

came home, I decided to go to Knoxville Business College. I was a secretary at Tennessee Mill and Mining, and then I went into the Navy for fifteen months. I was stationed at Bainbridge. Afterward, I settled in Baltimore because my aunt lived there and I'd visited her on weekends in the service.

"When I got out, there wasn't anything for me to do down home because there's nothing to do there, not even today. People had to go to Morristown or other places to get jobs. There wasn't anything available for me to do, so I took my service exam and started working for the federal government.

"So if people wanted to make money during the war, they would come up here to Baltimore because the jobs were so plentiful. They worked at Bethleham Steel Company, which was in shipbuilding, and with an airplane manufacturing business. They came up here by the truckloads. My brother came up here at that time too."[36]

Doman continued, "Though some graduates of the Vardy School stayed in the community after graduation, large numbers of them entered the working world outside the valley, moving off to larger towns and cities in Tennessee, where more employment opportunities existed. Maryland and Indiana in particular saw the establishment of small 'colonies' of Vardy folk. Former Vardy people moving to certain sections of Maryland, for example, maintain a network of social contacts including people who live in Sykesville, Frederick, Ellicott City, and parts of Baltimore. They sometimes refer among themselves to this geographical and social community as 'Little Hancock.' The sense of community is strong among them.

"Seven Gibson, a Baptist preacher who still lives in Vardy, takes a tent to Maryland every summer and holds a revival. When I asked him why he did this, he replied that he had grown 'tired of burying people he didn't know.' He explained that family connections to Vardy are so strong that people who were born in Maryland but whose parents were born in Vardy still form a distinct social group. These people often choose to be buried 'at home in the valley' rather than in the communities where they were born and had spent most of their lives. By traveling to Maryland to preach each year, Reverend Gibson honors and maintains the extended boundaries of this remarkable community and helps maintain the feeling of community

---

[36]Ruth J. Muhlbauer, telephone interview by DruAnna Overbay, 20 July 2002.

shared by a number of people who trace their roots to this tiny valley in the mountains of East Tennessee."[37]

After being asked why she had not left Tennessee, Geraldine Hatfield Bell explained, "My brothers, Buster, Kenneth, and Milburn, moved to Indiana to go into construction work, but I wanted to stay close to my parents. One of the most valuable pieces of advice that our parents taught us was for us to always pay our debts and treat people good. My dad was an honest man and a hard worker so he taught us how to work, too."[38]

Being honest, paying our debts, working hard, and treating people respectfully are lessons that interviewees thought were most important in earning a livelihood, no matter where they lived.

Proud of his new red wagon, my brother Dan and Dad show off the toy to Sunday-dinner guests: Aunt Jane Horton Watson, Papa Horton, Aunt Lorene Horton, Claribel Miser Horton, Aunt Maude Belle Williams, Mama, and Stella Miser. Papa and Claribel returned often from their Indiana home with their children Lorene and "Junior."

+ + + + +

Grandma's Trunk

Undisturbed the coal dust lay thick
Across the mantel's fireplace
Begriming three tintypes
Strewn across the floor
Bits and pieces of Grandma's life
Thirty years gone.
Uncle Chris's chubbiness
Ruddy, rotundity revealed

---

[37]Doman, manuscript.
[38]Geraldine Hatfield Bell, interviewed by DruAnna W. Overbay, Blountville TN, 19 August 2000.

Behind a long flaxen beard
Piercing blue eyes,
"Blue as a gander's,"
Grandma said.
Uncle Tom's suavity
In West Point's cadet uniform
Displayed his Captain's rank
Piercing blue eyes,
"Blue as a gander's"
Grandma said.
Uncle Nate's a dapper Dan,
gold-knobbed cane and top hat
Ascot astutely knotted
Piercing blue eyes,
"Blue as a gander's,"
Grandma said
One Williams brother's tintype missing
Grandpa's copy, handpainted years later,
Showed his red hair and handlebar moustache
Piercing blue eyes,
"Blue as a gander's,"
Grandma said.
Grandma's trunk scattered
And, there, with the tintypes,
A picture of me and on the back
Scrawled in shaky penmanship,
"Blue eyes,
Blue as a gander's"
Echoing through a memory
While swinging on the front porch
Holding me safely in her arms
Hearing it now—Grandma's voice,
Undisturbed the coal dust lies thick
Across the mantel's fireplace.

(Several years after Grandma's death.)

Chapter 11

School Days

"Prior to the construction of the first schoolhouse, educational efforts were centered in and around the home. Later, a few of the 'gifted' older children would take turns teaching. The first paid teachers would take turns boarding with the students' parents. School, then, was usually three to five months, depending on the weather and the crops," wrote W. P. Grohse, Jr.[1] School records beginning in the 1920s and 1930s document school as being 160 days per year as dictated by the state of Tennessee.

These young ladies, all cousins, were taught by Leham Collins and later tutored by the early missionaries. In front are Adelaide Collins and Carrie Collins. Behind them are Carrie's sisters, Docia and Laura.

My grandmother Adelaide and several of her cousins were tutored, we believe, by the early missionaries who boarded with her father Batey Collins. However, before the missionaries came, they had learned to read and write. One of the earliest photographs we have of my grandmother shows her wearing a first place ribbon and has written on the back that she graduated at the top of her class.

Ruth Jenkins Muhlbauer told us, "I remember my mommy telling me that the Presbyterians sent missionaries who taught during the school year and then would go back to their respective communities during the summer.

---

[1]W. P. Grohse, Jr., "A Brief History of Vardy Community, Hancock County," manuscript to Alyce and Drew Williams, Williams Family collection.

She went to school in the first schoolhouse and then later in the second schoolhouse. My grandfather Leham Collins taught school in the log schoolhouse which only went through the sixth grade."[2]

"Incidentally, Leham was my grandfather, and he met my grandmother, Carrie Collins, while teaching there. And, yes, they were cousins," Muhlbauer related to me.[3] Early Presbyterian missionaries wrote in journals that my great-uncle Noah Collins was also a teacher. How much education he had is unknown. Perhaps, he too had been taught by missionaries as had Grandma Adelaide.

It has been speculated that this first Vardy schoolhouse and meetinghouse was built before the Civil War. It remained in use until 1902.

The first schoolhouse was a one-room log cabin across the branch by the Bill Grohse residence. "That's where Clay Miser had a grist mill that my grandfather Howard Collins and his daughter Aunt Docia continued running after his death," said Muhlbauer.[4] The elder William P. Grohse bought the property and built his home there. By the late 1920s, the second schoolhouse, built in 1902 by the Presbyterians, was considered too small for the school's population, which had increased under the influence of teacher Miss Mary J. Rankin, who began her teaching career there shortly after her mission work began.

Miss Rankin was the first teacher in the area to have a college degree. The missionaries who came and went were the teachers and were paid by the Board of National Missions. There was no other school on the north

---

[2]Ruth Jenkins Muhlbauer, Vardy Oral Histories, interviewed by Katie Doman, Baltimore, March 2000, and Vardy Reunion, September 2000.

[3]Muhlbauer, telephone interview by DruAnna Overbay, 24 December 2004.

[4]Muhlbauer, telephone interview.

side of Newman's Ridge at that time. Others from surrounding communities began asking if they could be taught by Miss Rankin. Grohse stated that "As there was a great need for a school, she was given permission by the Hancock County Board of Education to teach school for four months with a salary of twenty-five dollars per month. She added two extra months for the older children who paid twenty-five cents per day. This was when women received 25 cents a day for field labor and men received 50. The tuition fees were paid from this work. The school board allowed her six dollars and a box of crayons for supplies. Even though Miss Rankin left Vardy in 1946, she is well remembered."[5]

Students from Vardy attended boarding schools in Hot Springs, North Carolina.

Another teacher who taught alongside Miss Rankin was Lewis Alder. He began teaching there in 1917. Having graduated from the McKinney Academy in Sneedville, Mr. Alder completed his education at Lincoln Memorial University in Harrogate, Tennessee, in 1913 with a certificate to teach. He became a member of the Vardy Community after marrying Rosa Mullins. They made their lifelong home in Vardy. Lewis Alder Williams remembered that "A copy of my grandfather's teaching contract hangs in the Vardy Church Museum, stating he was paid $50 for the five-month contract, providing the enrollment did not drop below twenty students. An

[5]Grohse, "A Brief History."

old family story has his disciplining the boys who acted up in class by having them stand on a wobbly three-legged table in the corner."[6]

The second Vardy school was constructed in 1902.

Miss Mary Rankin, far left, with students she taught in the 1902 school.

The earliest school registers that have been located were for the 1923–1924 school year and list Eva Mullins as one of the teachers. Records for 1925 indicate that Miss Rankin had been teaching there for six and a half years. Her Tennessee School Register for 1928 states that she attended elementary school in Stephen, Minnesota, and the Macalester Preparatory School in St. Paul, where she graduated in 1899. Four years later, in 1903, she got her B.A. degree from Macalester College before becoming a registered nurse. She received her M.A. from Columbia University in New York City.

Oakey Collins explained, "My first year at Vardy was the school year of the fall of 1928. That was the beginning of the new Vardy School; how-

---

[6]Lewis Alder Williams, "The Mail Carrier—Lewis Alder." *Vardy Voice.* August 2002.

ever, the new building had not been completed. The church was converted to serve as a schoolroom as well as to have church services. Grades fourth through the eighth attended school in the church."[7] The primary, first, second, and third grades attended school in Miss Rankin's cottage.

Students who attended Pease Home School, a boarding school in Asheville, and later went to Asheville Normal School were, on the front row, Helen Stewart, Mabel Stewart, Isa Mae Collins, and Zelma Collins. On the second row were Mossey (Aunt Jane) Horton and Mama with Aunt Nelle, their sister, immediately behind Mama. The other three are identified only as the Hopkins girls, who moved to Norton, Virginia.

Vardy's staff, pictured during the 1930s, included (front row) Josephine Leonard, Stella Miser, Eliza (Anderson) Goins, Ida "Mother" Leonard, and Mary J. Rankin. In back are Reverend Chester F. Leonard, Drew B. Williams, and William "Father" Leonard.

Cleland Collins added, "I attended the Vardy School in the school years beginning in the falls of 1928, 1929, 1930, and 1931. The new school was not ready for occupancy until the fall of 1929, so the church building was modified to serve as a school and church for the classes four through eight.

---

[7]Oakey Hendrix Collins, Vardy Oral Histories, interviewed by DruAnna Overbay, Morristown TN, 25 August 1999.

I believe that the one-room log schoolhouse that had previously been used before the 1902 school was used for the other grades."[8]

Actually, the second schoolhouse had been sold to William ("Bill") and Lillian Grohse. They converted it into their home by making several modifications to the building. The site of the log schoolhouse was later sold to Bill's parents, who moved down from New York City, and they built a new home on that site.

Miss Rankin and Preacher Leonard have taken their students to the construction site of their new school, which opened shortly after this picture was taken.

When the second school could no longer provide the space for the students to be properly educated, other arrangements were made. C. F. Leonard reported, "One day the 'preacher' announced that school would open in the church on Monday and that all who came had to bring something for tuition; everything useful would be acceptable. One man who offered a 'possum was told to send his children. Not a child reported to the county school. All came to us. As a result, after a little worry and work, the county gave us the salary for the teacher. This amounted to $200 a term and was used to provide books for the children, maps, tables, and desks. . . . Our

[8]Cleland Collins, Vardy Oral Histories, interviewed by Sally Collins and DruAnna Overbay, Morristown TN, 25 April 1999.

enrollment doubled and finally tripled until we are using the school building, two rooms in the church, one room in the mission home for homemaking classes, and a temporary building for manual training. We have two half-time teachers and one who teaches all day. We also have a manual training teacher and one for homemaking. Our attendance averaged 97 percent of the enrollment during the last term."[9]

In October 1928, Chester F. Leonard reported that the students were occupying the new school. The building was incomplete but was finished during 1929, when it was dedicated to the Vardy Community. Here students are shown returning from recess followed by their teacher. Not on the left the stack of wood that had been prepared for the winter months. Benches on the right served as an outdoor classroom as well as for community gatherings on warm Sunday afternoons.

After Reverend Leonard saw that a new school building had become a necessity, he began formulating ideas for its construction and made a proposition to the community that a new school would be built if the people would donate enough lumber. "Eleven thousand feet were offered and rejected. The meeting adjourned and the men got together. The next day

---

[9]C. F. Leonard, "Helping a Community Help Itself," *The Presbyterian Advance*, 18 October 1928.

two men came and begged for a two-weeks' extension. As a result the community gave 60,000 feet of pine and oak lumber, besides some of the labor. The building is going up right now."[10]

Miss Mary Rankin gathers her students for a classroom demonstration, which included student involvement, a favorite class-time routine.

Patiently working with her students, Miss Rankin monitors their progress as they complete their individual "seat work."

The minister's mother, Ida Leonard, whom the children affectionately called "Mother Leonard," teaches Gladys Miser dressmaking skills.

Carefully thought-out plans by the "preacher" included "a large department for farm-repair training, woodworking, dressmaking, home nursing,

---

[10]Leonard, "Helping a Community Help Itself."

etiquette, etc.; rooms for regular classwork; and a special experimental room where we shall try new methods of teaching of 'peculiar' minds. This room will be equipped with picture machines, experimental tables, and other special devices for teaching those who find book learning especially difficult. An assembly room will be built for lectures, exhibits, and plays. There will be rooms for teachers, a restroom with a first-aid section, and a well-selected library."[11]

School Campus and Building

Vardy Presbyterian Community School campus encompassed seven acres. In addition to the school building were the carriage house/horse stable (garage), woodshed/blacksmith shop, summer home, dairy, chicken house, well house, fountain house, and three playgrounds. The acreage had been donated by Batey Collins. After Batey's death in 1914, two of his daughters and sons-in-laws, Daniel Boone and Adelaide Collins Horton and Logan and Nancy Collins Miser, released additional acreage to the Presbyterians. The last half acre was sold for one dollar in April, 1926. All of the acreage had been part of Vardemon Collins's properties.

Ruth Muhlbauer related that "During the construction of the new schoolhouse, the supplies, such as seats, desks, and blackboards, had to be hauled from the railroad station in Ben Hur, Virginia. The men in the community hauled them in on wagons because they didn't have any trucks back in those days. Of course, the people in the community who had given timber for the construction had to cut the trees, take them to the saw mill, and then haul the boards up to the school."

When the new school was being constructed, the community people were amazed at its enormity and space. The massive three-story building, set on the Powell Mountain side overlooking the church, was ready for all students during the summer of 1929. Students who had been attending classes in the Rankin cottage and the church were anxious to explore their new surroundings and were in awe at the changes.[12]

A dedication service for the new school was held on November 28, 1929. At that time Reverend Leonard presented his report of the annual business meeting. He began, "This has been a great year for us in our

---

[11]Leonard, "Helping a Community Help Itself."
[12]Ruth Jenkins Muhlbauer, telephone interviews by DruAnna Overbay, July 2002.

community at Vardy. At no time in the history of our community have we had so many things to be grateful for."[13]

Even though this was Thanksgiving Day, he stated in the report, "Of course, there are certain things that have harmed us and held us back from being the best that we could have been." He mentioned three major disappointments: adversity to change, distrust and criticism, and the sadness of death, illness, and unchristian behavior.

However, Leonard quickly dispensed the "everything isn't perfect mood" to a more joyful one in keeping with the season, saying, "But, today we wish to count our blessings." In the five major blessings he mentioned, the first was that the new school building had been completed and the equipment was in use. This section of the report offers clarity to some of the oral histories, which at times confuse facts and dates.

"You people," Leonard concluded, "helped wonderfully with your words of advice and with your giving of lumber. To you we hope will come a full appreciation of the value of this building, and for you we hope to provide much pleasure through its use."[14] No doubt a full appreciation and much pleasure by those who had the privilege of attending Vardy School is evident today in the efforts of the Vardy Community Historical Society.

The VCHS and those interviewed for this oral history are ever mindful of the impact the school has had on their lives and have expressed a desire to show that appreciation to those whom Preacher Leonard mentioned in his service on that day. "Friends in the North very kindly provided the money that we needed. We wish that they could be with us today to see how we are using what they have provided and to more fully understand its great place in our lives. Miss Rankin and I can best appreciate all that has been accomplished. At first, we used the old school and the little library room. Then, we used the old school, library room, and large church room. Later, we added Miss Rankin's house for homemaking and the store for manual training. Now, we have this building with charts, maps, chairs, tables, lights, pictures, organ, and all of the equipment that we need."[15]

As a 1929 student, Cleland Collins remembered thinking that the building was rather large: "It had windows all the way around the outside on every floor. The ground level contained manual training and woodworking shops. . . . The second floor was used as classrooms. As I

---

[13]Vardy Community Presbyterian Church Records.

[14]Vardy Community Presbyterian Church Records.

[15]Vardy Community Presbyterian Church Records.

remember, there were four classrooms and an assembly room. . . . Father and Mother Leonard used the third floor as their living quarters; however, all levels were available or could be used, if need be, for classes. Each level could be entered from the outside. . . . We also had a 110-volt generator electric plant."

"Chester Leonard had gone to Nashville long before I got there and took a course in heat power. He developed a Delco system which ran by a gas generator and then the charge went into wet batteries, over against dry cells, and the energy was stored there in these wet batteries and then drawn out for illumination."[16]

Illumination for the classrooms was provided by the generator, but just having a new school lit up the lives of students for many years. Their pride in the school is still evident today. "Vardy was the most beautiful school in the whole county. . . . On the first day that I went, I could see it was so big that I thought I'd never be able to get through that school. . . . It was a very big school. It was one of the finest schools in the county at that time," Lloyd Williams bragged.[17]

As a matter of fact, when the school was built, it was considered the state of the art in design and construction. At that time it was practically unheard of for a rural mountain school in Tennessee to have more than one room. People in the community often boasted that their school had ninety-six windows. Indeed it did, for Reverend Leonard wished to harness the sun's energy not only to keep the building with sufficient light but also heat. In the summer and early fall months, the windows stayed open, creating cross ventilation through the hallways and classrooms.

Entrance to the lower level of the three-story structure was across a rock stoop beneath the front entrance porch. Inside, stairs going to the second level were on the right. Beneath the stairs was a cloakroom with pegs for students to hang their coats and hats. To the left was Miss Rankin's primer (primary) and first-grade classroom. Further down the hall was the library. At the end of the hallway, one entered a large classroom, which housed the manual training and woodworking (shop) classroom, where William Leonard, affectionately called Father Leonard, taught. To the right of the classroom was a screened area that went under the rest of the school, where tools and lumber were stored. Projecting from two large

[16]David F. Swartz, "They Came. They Stayed," manuscript given to Vardy Community Historical Society, June 2001.

[17]Lloyd Williams, Vardy Oral Histories.

double doors behind the shop was a rock porch that was beneath the second floor's back-door porch. After the school enrollment decreased during the 1940s, the library was extended into Miss Rankin's classroom.

The main entrance took one up five or six rock steps to a covered porch over which a large sign proclaimed "Vardy Community School." Entering the large hallway, one saw a double staircase leading to the third floor. On the right were the classrooms for the sixth, seventh, and eighth grades, which Mr. Leonard taught.

The second and third grades were in a classroom to the left, where Miss Gleason taught. At the end of the hallway was a large auditorium with stationary folding auditorium seats. Directly in front was Mr. Leonard's classroom. The auditorium had a movie screen and a stage, which was on a hinged platform, beneath which props for plays could be housed. On the right wall were cupboards to store audiovisual equipment. The left wall had a number of large windows, which had dark shades that could be drawn. To the left of the auditorium in the short hall was my dad's classroom, where he taught fourth and fifth grades. Directly in front of that classroom's door were the steps from the lower level, which opened behind a door. The fourth and fifth grade classroom had one wall made of folding doors so that the auditorium could be expanded. Large double doors from the classroom took one out to the covered back porch, down rock steps, and up the paths to the playgrounds.

On the third floor, a large hallway ran the length of the building. When one crossed the hall directly in front of the stairs, a large lunchroom with long tables and portable folding chairs provided space for students to have lunch. Later hot lunches would be served there. The lunchroom had a large wood-burning cookstove and a large double sink with running water on the front right wall. Large windows like those throughout the school ran the width of the back wall. A back door to the right of the cafeteria provided a fire escape route, which led to a sun porch and then onto the catwalk.

The end of the hall housed living quarters for Mother and Father Leonard, which consisted of a combined kitchen, dining area and living room, and a bedroom that opened into a large storage area and into Mother Leonard's classroom, complete with sewing machines, where she taught home economics. Sewing machines could easily be stored in the large storage area so that folding rollaway cots could be placed in the classroom for overnight guests. Behind the Leonards' living quarters was the catwalk that extended the breadth of the lower walkway. "It emerged onto the adjoining hill where the dairy and summer house, where Mother and Father

Leonard lived in the summer, were located. Also a sheep pen and chicken house were there," Dan explained.[18]

Recalling sheep stories, Swartz told me, "We did have sheep, and I think it was kind of a hobby that Mr. Leonard had. . . . We had a couple of ewes that had been bred, and later on we got a ram. It was a good strain. . . . Mr. Leonard got up so early . . . around 4:00 in the morning, and he came over to see me around 5:30 one morning that it had been raining. . . . and, he said, 'Good afternoon.' I thought for a city boy that was pretty early . . . and he continued, 'We have a dead ram, and I wondered if you'd take care of it.' I asked, 'Are you going to shear it?' He said, 'No.' I asked, 'We can't reclaim any of the food?' He replied, 'No!'

"So that morning I went up and dug a pit, a pretty good-sized one, and lifted that carcass in, covered it up . . . and, about two weeks later it had to be done again for another. So I said, 'I don't believe these are too healthy.' He said, 'I don't either.' He did get some others, and they did shear them. I don't think that he ever butchered any of them.

"The purpose for those sheep was to keep the grass cut. We had to pen them up when the ewes were healthy enough to bear lambs. Then there was this weaning process. I had to help separate the lambs from their mothers, and, of course, the noise and the bleating of those sheep were really something. It was hard to sleep because they were right in the backyard."[19]

Robert Moore lamented, "The school grounds always looked as if they'd just been mowed because of those sheep. One of the things that was so amazing to me was how beautiful that schoolhouse was. It was such a treasure. And it's such a loss for the community and everybody involved that it cannot be restored."[20]

In 1934, Reverend Leonard wrote, "Our property is in better condition than ever before. The new well, which took so long to build, is dug twenty feet into the solid rock, cemented and tiled so that not a drop of water can get in unless it goes through several feet of blue limestone rock. The well house is built, and the siphon system of getting water is installed. This is the first year of school that we have not had to carry water. Although the well was completed after the setting in of dry weather, we have had enough

---

[18]D. H. Williams, Vardy Oral Histories, interviewed by DruAnna Overbay, 15 June 2002.

[19]Swartz, Vardy Oral Histories.

[20]Robert Moore, Vardy Oral Histories, interviewed by DruAnna Overbay, Talbott TN, 13 July 2002.

water for our use. Retaining walls have been built where needed. The woodland has been cleared and is really beautiful. I wish to thank Dewey Collins for his faithfulness and his fine work during the many days when we needed him."[21]

All of those interviewed felt that they had benefited greatly from their experiences at Vardy School. R. C. Mullins stated that as a child he saw it as a place of beginning: "It was a place of learning, a place where people cared about people. For me, it was a starting out in life when we were coming off that ridge."[22]

"Had it not been for Vardy Community School and Church, I would have never been able to see the need of an education," declared W. C. Collins, now a retired teacher. "I owe my life to that great institution."[23]

Several children are lined up, waiting their turns to use the swings on either side of the lower playground. Below the rock wall was the middle playground and above the rock wall was the ballfield and playground for the upper grades.

School Play Areas

Reverend Leonard wrote, "The playground is a source of delight to all of us. It is in use five days every week, and sometimes six. The men who worked there should be very proud of what they have done. There is

---

[21] Vardy Community Presbyterian Church Records.

[22] R. C. Mullins, Vardy Oral Histories, interviewed by DruAnna Overbay, Talbott TN, 15 June 2002.

[23] W. C. Collins, Vardy Oral Histories, interviewed by Katie Doman, Sneedville TN, 7 August 2000.

nothing like it anywhere around and will not be for some years to come. The leveling off of the ground has done much to improve the usefulness of the place. Also enlarging the ballfield has made a much better place to play. The grounds are now adequately large for our needs for years to come. I have new swing equipment on the way now so that we can put up chains in place of the rope swings for the little children and thus add to the general attractiveness and safety of the place. With balls, trolleys, swings, and other apparatuses, our children are very happy and satisfied."[24]

Lively horseshoe competitions were held during school hours and also on Saturday and Sunday afternoons for everyone in the community.

Dave Swartz, on the right, observes a Saturday afternoon horseshoe tournament between Vardy School students.

Three levels of the playground were located on the hill directly behind the school. Oakey Collins remembered the playground during the early years as having only two levels: "One was possibly four to six feet higher than the other. They were leveled off with a horse and what we called a pan that would haul dirt from one place to another to dump it."[25]

---

[24]Leonard, Vardy Community Presbyterian Church Records.
[25]Oakey Collins.

The outdoor restrooms were located in the far corner of the lower area. A row of swings was reserved for the students in the lower grades, and another row of swings on the opposite side of the playground was for the students in the middle grades. Two seesaws and slides were on the north side of the area. One section was reserved for the younger children and the taller section for older students. "We have a large playground with swings, seesaws and horseshoes. The little children use these things," wrote Geraldine Davidson.[26]

Having my teeth nearly knocked out was one of the worst memories that I have of the playground. One of the boys knew how to push down on the seesaw just as we walked by it to make the opposite side hit us hard. One day he convinced me that he would seesaw with me, and just as I started to get on, he pushed his side down so that it caught me right under my chin. It upset me so badly that I slugged him. Of course, I got a paddling for my unladylike conduct. But, there are so many other good memories of swinging with my favorite cousins Billie Clyde and Georgia Ruth Mullins and my other friends Kate Mullins, Tootsie Hatfield, Deanna Moore, Ollie Faye Johnson, Beulah Gibson, Dennis Trent, Harold Roberts, Black Boy Gibson, and Sallie Bee Hatfield. There were other friends whose faces I can see, but whose names I can't remember. We had such a good time and always took turns and never really had many arguments about who got to swing longer. I remember that Dennis Trent kept us from going over our time limit. He had us count the times we pushed the swings, and after so many pushes when the swing slowed down, we had to get off.

The second level was reserved for students in the fourth through eighth grades. The main attraction there was the horseshoe pits. Lloyd Williams recalled, "Pitching horseshoes was a big thing then. . . . We always looked forward to it. . . . if we got good enough to pitch horseshoes, then we were attracted to that game because of how well we could do, and we wanted to be there all the time."[27]

Horseshoe games are also remembered by Leonard Gibson, who wrote, "I always looked forward to playing horseshoes. Euna Trent and I were always partners, and most of the time we would win!"[28]

---

[26]Geraldine Davidson, *Vardy School Newspaper* article. Scrapbook of Vardy Principal Mossie Kate Overton, 1942–1945.

[27]Lloyd Williams, Vardy Oral Histories.

[28]Leonard Gibson, "Remembering Vardy School," manuscript given to interviewer Katie Doman, Baltimore MD, 6 March 2000.

Swartz reminisced, "Part of my job in the afternoon, maybe on a weekend, would be to supervise the horseshoe matches. Usually they were doubles, and it was a big deal. We would keep track of the score, had some little beads or something like that to keep track of the points. One time I was invited to a party in Sneedville, and I didn't have much in the way of a social life, but didn't need a lot, I guess. . . . That Saturday afternoon I wanted to go into Sneedville so I asked Mr. Leonard if I could go, and he said, 'But, David, horseshoes,' meaning that I had a horseshoe assignment in the afternoon, so I didn't go. I had to be there with the horseshoes and the young people who enjoyed that. By the way, Chester Leonard was a pretty good horseshoe player, and I learned to play, not as well, but I enjoyed it."[29]

Competitions among the students were held often and were reported in the area newspaper. According to Betty Mullins, "The best horseshoe pitchers were Edward Mullins, Miss Overton, Mae Williams, and Josephine Moore."[30]

Oakey Collins recalled the upper playground, or third level, as having the trolley and two swings, made out of hemp rope tied onto trees, one on the west side and one on the northeast side of the playground. "We would swing out over a well house that was on the lower part. . . . We also had a slide built out of wood and tin as well as a sled that we would pull back up the hill and, of course, they kept that greased so that we could ride down. It was a roller coaster type thing. I remember that I was the first one to discover that on the rope swings if I ran hard enough and held my feet way up, I could go all the way around until the rope twisted its way up. I played softball . . . and Drew Williams, one of the teachers, played with us and took part in our activities."[31]

Being old enough to go up to the third level of the playground was a big event for most students because the ballfield, trolleys, and rope swing were located there. "When we got in the sixth or maybe seventh grade, we would get to go to the big playground where we played softball. I remember playing football. We'd all choose sides, and we had to kick the ball or take it to the goal by kicking it. We couldn't touch it with our hands, but we'd kick it. Our shins and legs would get torn up," laughed R. C. Mullins.[32]

---

[29]Swartz, Vardy Oral Histories.
[30]Betty Mullins. *Vardy School Newspaper* article.
[31]O. H. Collins.
[32]R. C. Mullins.

Lloyd Williams said, "We had a game called soccer. Played it with a football."[33]

Other fun activities were remembered by Charles Sizemore. "We had a trolley that we'd ride. It was hooked up on a cable between two trees with a pulley, and we could ride down that trolley. We had to pull it back up the hill with a rope. There was always a softball game going on. Sometimes we would invent games, and we played marbles."[34]

"We had a couple of trolleys behind the ballfield that when you got to be in the fifth or sixth grade you would get to ride," explained my brother.[35]

Older students wait in line to ride on the "trolley," the subject of many playground memories.

"The trolley was a heavy wire with a pulley tied to one big tree and coming down a decline over a little ravine and onto another tree. That was a source of a lot of pleasure as well as a few accidents," said Swartz.[36]

"The trolley was my favorite thing to get on and ride. I always liked to ride the trolley. . . . When I got out on the playground, I was never too much involved because I was a dreamer. I was never into sports or playing ball or anything like that because I couldn't compete," stated Moore.[37]

Swartz added, "There was a lot of good competition, and the boys and girls played together . . . on teams they would choose or be chosen for. . . .

---

[33]Lloyd Williams.
[34]Sizemore.
[35]D. H. Williams.
[36]Swartz.
[37]Moore.

The one thing that they enjoyed was kicking a football since we didn't have a soccer ball. We made up our own rules, or they did, and I would watch them and try to stay out of their way since those legs started kicking each other. The main focus for that lot was softball. Mr. Leonard would be up there for the softball games. He was always the pitcher and in charge of the ballgames. He enjoyed that because he felt that his pitching made it more equal. He pitched consistently in the same way for both sides. It was a lot of fun in that some of the girls were extremely good hitters and fielders, and I tried to take my position and enjoy the game."[38]

Not only did the students enjoy baseball and softball on the upper playground but the residents of the community who gathered there on Sunday afternoons also enjoyed the camaraderie.

"The most interesting thing for us older students was the baseball game. We got to choose sides each week," Davidson wrote.[39]

A red-faced Audrey Franz told us, "I loved to play baseball and volleyball . . . I could hit the baseball pretty hard and I could run like crazy. . . . We were up there playing one Saturday, girls and boys. My team was winning. . . . then it was my time to bat. So I batted the ball and it went flying. I ran about halfway to second base . . . when my underwear came down. . . . My underwear was so big, Mommy had put a pin in it. That pin came loose, and my underwear started coming down to my knees. I had to go down to the toilet. I was too embarrassed, and I thought they wouldn't even let me play with them anymore. It made me so angry that I cried and cried. . . .

"When I got home, I was still crying, 'My, my pin,' I told Mommy, 'If you ever put a pin in my underwear again . . . ' and I sat on the porch crying. . . . I guess it hurt Mommy's feelings, too. I can't remember ever having to put a pin in my underwear after that . . . I think she went to the

---

[38]Swartz.
[39]Geraldine Davidson, *Vardy School Newspaper* article.

store and got some elastic and wove through them . . . but, after that pin came loose, I lost my interest in baseball."[40]

The rope swing took older students over a steep hill and demanded that one hold on tightly to avoid falling. Many students couldn't wait for their turns to challenge their endurance.

"While playing on the playground, my slip straps broke, and my slip fell to the ground! All of the children laughed and pointed at me," wrote Glessie Collins Cummings in response to her most embarrassing remembrance at Vardy.[41]

And Thomas Collins recalled, "There was a big oak tree on the back side of the upper playground. It had a big rope that we hung onto to swing to the other side of the hill. Sometimes if the teacher wasn't watching, two or three of us would get on and swing across. Occasionally it would break; but, we came out all right, with just a handful of scrapes and bruises and a bunch of good memories."[42]

In addition to the third level, there was a small area adjacent to the ballfield with a volleyball court. Swartz recalled, "I helped a little bit in leveling out what was a volleyball court area. It was part of the hill, and we took a team of mules or at least one good draft horse with a scoop behind it. After we pulverized the ground a little bit, we tried to scoop out some of it and level it off to make a flat area. It was another flat area in addition to the baseball field, which was already done before I got here. So we had this one large area, then a raised portion, and another one for the volleyball. Between the two we had this trolley."[43]

---

[40]Franz.

[41]Glessie Collins Cummins, Vardy Community School Reunion Questionnaire, 4 September 2004.

[42]Thomas Collins, Vardy Oral Histories, interviewed by Sally Collins, West Liberty KY, 21 June 2002.

[43]Swartz.

"The playgrounds with the swings and trolleys were so memorable!" said Glessie Collins Cummins.[44]

Finally, Thomas Collins recalled, "We had a good playground at Vardy. It was well kept and always clean. By clean, I mean that the rocks and sticks were picked up because in nice weather we were in our bare feet!"[45]

Often students would gather either to walk or ride their horses to and from school. These residents are returning to their homes toward the Virginia line after a community meeting.

On the first day, some parents walked their children to school to make sure they were properly enrolled.

School Transportation

"We lived one mile east of the school and walked there. However, there were kids who lived four or five miles from school. Some of them walked, and some of them rode horses. The school provided a roofed hitching post for the horses," said Cleland Collins.[46]

Muhlbauer explained, "We had no public transportation, and we went to school whether it was raining or snow was up to our knees. Sometimes

[44]Cummings.
[45]Thomas Collins.
[46]Cleland Collins.

it was so cold that one of the men in the community would get up early to have a fire going in his fireplace so we kids could come in and warm our feet on the way to school. At other times our feet would be so cold that when we got to school, Miss Rankin would make us take off our stockings, put our feet in snow, and sit by the stove until the water thawed because one shouldn't warm up frozen feet too fast. We had two and a half miles to walk to school. For a six-year-old kid that was a long walk. The roads were so rocky, and there were no bridges over the branches. When it would rain in the springtime, the branches would fill up so high with water that the older kids would have to take off their shoes and carry the younger ones across because the water was rapid."[47]

Saddling up in front of Ruth Anderson's, a student named Lonnie rode the family mule to school. Note the paling fence atop stacked rocks which many families in the 1920s and 1930s used around their houses and gardens to keep out stray animals.

After returning from Asheville Farm School, Darnell Williams was hired by the community to provide bus transportation for the students to and from Vardy School.

Walking to school seemed to be the surest mode of transportation since there were no school buses running during the first twenty years of the privately owned church school, a no-fee school for those in the Vardy Valley. Going to school during the mid-1930s, W. C. Collins had lived on Newman's Ridge, and he said, "We walked to school at Vardy. That was

<hr>

[47]Mulhbauer interview.

about two and one-half miles each way. We very seldom missed a day. All of the children attended there until they finished eighth grade."[48]

Another Newman's Ridge resident who didn't live quite as far out the ridge from the school was R. C. Mullins, who remembered the walk from the school to his home taking him about twenty or thirty minutes. "We seldom missed. Sometimes when it rained really hard and the valley would flood, we would go out to the bluff and yell down to Drew Williams, who lived below us in the valley, to see if the footlog was covered with water. If it were, we wouldn't go to school that day, but if the water was just up real high, Drew or D. H. would come and help us make our way across," remembered R. C. Mullins.[49]

If a student were able to get to the forks of Mulberry Gap-Sneedville Road, a church-school bus from the McKinney Presbyterian Academy took them on into Sneedville.

Leonard Gibson wrote, "We lived on top of Newman's Ridge and walked down the ridge every day for eight years. My brothers, sister, and I walked each day with Ralph, Ellis, Betty, and R. C. Mullins and also Rosa Lee Goins and her brothers. I don't remember any of us complaining about having to walk down the ridge and back up. I remember walking to school barefooted with frost on the ground. We had to walk across the creek on a log just behind Drew Williams' barn. Sometimes the log was pretty slick. When it rained, the water would rise—that was when we got to leave school early. I remember Mossy Mullins, our cousin, would walk down to the creek with us to make sure we made it across. On top of the ridge, our mom was watching us walk that log, too. The water was very deep and dangerous."[50]

---

[48]W. C. Collins, Vardy Oral Histories, interviewed by Katie Doman, Sneedville TN, 7 August 2000.

[49]R. C. Mullins.

[50]Leonard Gibson.

Having moved from one home to another, walking to school for Charles Sizemore was no more than a mile's distance from either house. Sizemore said that "Darnell Williams was contracted before there was a bus to haul the kids who had to come from longer distances. From the forks of the road to the Virginia line, he would haul the ones who came the longest distances, but the ones who lived a mile or a mile and a half always walked. Darnell had a truck with a kind of homemade camper that he built on the back that he used to haul students. Of course, a lot of them had to walk across the ridge and mountain down to the road, where he would pick them up."[51]

Jean Sizemore joined Luigene and Mae Williams as a freshman at Hancock County in the fall of 1945.

Mae Williams was proud to be one of the three students entering Hancock County High School as freshmen.

Students who lived on Newman's Ridge came from different sections of the ridge. Those living directly above the church and school did not have a chance to ride with Darnell Williams. Those who lived on the west and east of the church walked down to the valley road to catch a ride with him. Johnnie Gibson Rhea remembered that "He [Williams] drove a pickup truck with a cattle rack that he had covered with tar paper for us to have a shelter from the cold and rain. There were benches around the bed where we sat. Sometimes we fought on it and got angry with Darnell for making us behave. One day we decided that we would tear his tar paper cover.

"Those who would not go along with our destroying his cover we threatened to make them eat a piece of the tar paper. We would say, 'Tear a piece or eat a piece.' We tore the cover completely up. The next day Mr. Leonard talked to all of us and told us that we each would have to bring a dime to school to pay for the cover's replacement. I refused to pay the dime

---

[51]Sizemore.

and quit going to Vardy over a dime. It was the biggest mistake I made for my education. I learned more at Vardy than in any other school I went to."[52]

Luigene Williams, along with three other Vardy students, entered the freshman year in high school at Hancock County High School.

One of the first Vardy students to graduate from Hancock County High School was W. C. Collins. He transferred from Warren Wilson in Swannanoa, N.C. after the roads had been improved in 1945.

Audrey Mullins Franz said, "I don't even know how many miles it was, but I had to come out the ridge to the road and come all the way down the ridge and then all the way to the school. . . . And you know how I got there? Walked, honey. Padded my little feet right on the ground. . . . Finally, when Helen Mullins started teaching, they got a bus. . . . What in the world was his name? He was a man with a . . . like a jeep. He would haul us to school. . . . When he started driving that like a jeep bus, we all would have to walk out in the ridge road to catch that jeep. I was so glad when Helen Mullins got to be a teacher because I didn't have to walk up and down the valley road anymore. We still had to walk down to the bottom and back up the ridge road."[53]

It wasn't until 1946 that Vardy got its first school bus, which ran a route from the Virginia line to the forks of the road. "We had a little bit of trouble getting to school since we lived so far away from where the bus ran. Many times the bus would tear up and we'd have to walk. Of course, we always got to school.

Robert Moore remembered, "Why, it wasn't so bad walking except during the winter. We never had many shoes except during the winter, and sometimes they were in pretty bad shape. I can remember, when I lived not too far from the school, sitting on a rock waiting on the school bus and

---

[52]Johnnie Gibson Rhea, Vardy Oral Histories, interviewed by Katie Doman, Sneedville TN, 10 August 2000.

[53]Audrey Mullins Franz, Vardy Oral Histories, interviewed by Katie Doman, Baltimore MD, March 2000.

raising my feet up one at a time to let the sun shine on them to get them warm"[54]

Students who had graduated from Vardy could meet another bus at the forks of the road to take them on into Sneedville, where they attended Hancock County High School.

Before that time, Claribel Miser related that the old rickety church-school bus took some of the students over the treacherous ridge to Sneedville to the McKinney Academy, a three-year Presbyterian high school that later became Hancock County High School. "I didn't want to ride that old bus because it had bad brakes, and I cried not to go. Finally, my mama told me that I didn't have to go. Maybe that is why I decided to drive a school bus when Dan and I moved to Indiana."[55]

Feeling that the new high school did not meet their needs and that others considered them inferior led students who wanted to further their education to be sent to Presbyterian-affiliated boarding schools. Ralph Goins and others attended the Asheville Farm School for boys while a few of the girls went to Dorland Bell.

Later, many went on to Warren Wilson, both a high school and a junior college. When public education first began in the county, many of the children in Vardy were not permitted to attend the white schools because of being considered Melungeon. That was a reality that my mother faced. Her father D. B. Horton provided an education for his children by sending them to boarding schools in Asheville, North Carolina.

My sister Charlotte Williams went to Warren Wilson during her freshman year but became ill and had to come home, where she attended Hancock County off and on during her illness. My older brother went to Hancock County High School but spent two years at Knoxville High School, where he graduated. Margaret went all four years to Hancock County. They all rode the bus to Hancock High, and so did I until we moved to Knoxville.

When we moved, I continued my education at Powell High School. After graduation I joined my cousins Mickey (Melissa Jane), Billie, and Georgia Mullins at Warren Wilson. Education was stressed by our families since both my mother and Helen Mullins, their mother, were teachers.

---

[54]Moore, Vardy Oral Histories.

[55]Claribel Miser Horton, Vardy Oral Histories, interviewed by DruAnna W. Overbay, Seymour IN, 17 July 1999.

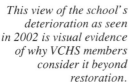

This view of the school's deterioration as seen in 2002 is visual evidence of why VCHS members consider it beyond restoration.

+ + + + +

School Days 1947—1954

Unique to the Hancock County hills
of East Tennessee,
Vardy Presbyterian School, built in 1928—
Three-storied Colossus sitting on
Great-grandpa Batey's land
Educated the Melungeon children for fifty years
Time ripping the tin roof, rain dripping on the oaken floors,
Vandals stripping the bell tower, the library shelves,
The museum's contents, the classroom furniture
Wind shifting the structure, fallen in disarray.
Father Leonard taught woodworking
Shop, on the lower level, behind the library
Hammering sawing lawn and porch chairs,
Cutting out wooden boys in overalls and girls in sunbonnets
Middle level's auditorium slumping,
Stretching Twain's tales to innocent ears
Flanking all sides, the classrooms—
Miss Rankin's primer class reciting "ABC's"
And Bible verses read in Scottish dialect
Mama's first and second graders gathered around tables
Reading "Spot, Dick, and Jane," making colored chalk paste
Dipping sycamore balls to hang on Christmas trees
Cutting construction paper tulips
         and daffodils for spring windows

Third and fourth graders becoming proficient in multiplication,
Additions, subtraction, division,
    fractions under Mrs. Mullins' tutelage
Fifth and sixth graders singing insolent taunts to Mr. Hoye Brown
"Going to town, riding a Billy goat, leading a hound,"
Running through the halls escaping Daddy's paddle
Seventh and eighth graders learning Tennessee history,
Diagramming sentence structures, science classifications,
Listening to a reading of Poe's "The Gold Bug"
Upper level cafeteria cornbread baking,
    soup beans, mustard greens,
Government cheese, butter, peanut butter
Aunt Lizzie and Lit Mammy's powdered sugar
    and cornflakes candy
Museum housed missionary's souvenirs
    from China, Japan, and the Navajos
Mother Leonard's home economics' classes,
    sewing machines humming
Ruffle-tailed skirts sewn from feed-sack material
Clothing ribboned, puckered, sashed,
    belted in tiny rosebud patterns
Visiting teacher's quarters, nearby Mother and Father Leonard's
Out the back windows, the pump and well houses
Bubbling waters flowing through drinking fountains
Lower playground swings and seesaws in a rhythmic tandem
Middle playground horseshoes rebounding
Upper playground baseballs and softballs thrown
Amid the trolley's slide across the hillside
Out the front windows, below the school
Preacher Leonard opened his first-aid clinic,
Checking heads for lice, fingers for itch, oozing sores, pinkeye
Attended Johns Hopkins Medical School, this preacher man
More than ministered to his flock there at
Vardy Community's Presbyterian School,
Unique to the Hancock County hills of East Tennessee.

(After Vardy's first school reunion, 1996)

Chapter 12

School Curriculum

The basic three Rs were a part of the everyday curriculum at Vardy, but more importantly the Presbyterian Church school taught the three Rs of morals—Respect, Responsibility, and Religion—throughout the curriculum. Bible classes were an integral part of the instruction, coordinated with lessons involving proper social behavior and service to the school in work-related activities. Learning to read and write were emphasized in the primary, first, and second grades. Math instruction also began early. Most students had mastered their multiplication facts by the third grade. Geography, history, agriculture, vocational courses, health, first aid, and physical education were all part of the course work. An additional class period for library activities, during which children were allowed to choose books for both silent and oral reading activities, encouraged reading for enjoyment. A library such as Vardy's was rare in rural schools and non-existent in area schools.

Children who lived on farms that bordered the church and school campus often played together after school and on weekends. This group includes Charles Sizemore, Charlotte Williams, Dan Williams, Jean Sizemore, Margaret Williams, and Leona Moore.

As a result, many within the county who envied Vardy's program tried to dictate how the school should be run. Since the school was a private church school that enjoyed state support through partial funding of the teachers' salaries, Preacher Leonard took his argument to the state to avoid further attempts within the county to take away state support. Leonard's 1934 annual report reflects the results.

In May, having been nagged so long by different parties who were trying to tell us how this school had to be run and feeling that now was the time to settle things, I made a trip to Nashville, where I conferred with the Commissioner, his assistant, the directors of high schools and elementary schools, and there settled for our community the standing of this school. At Nashville the following statements were made:

1. The Vardy School shall be allowed to experiment in its own way with no state hindrances as to textbooks, equipment, or methods requirements. It shall be considered the laboratory school for that Eastern section of rural work in Tennessee and shall be unhampered.

2. The Vardy School, being so far in advance of the other county schools, should not submit its pupils to countywide examinations. The teaching at Vardy does not embrace textbooks only but supplementary materials. Therefore, to require county examinations would mean a return to itemized material found only in textbooks, some of which is many years out of date.

3. The State is very glad to consider Vardy as a County School and hopes to have its cooperation in the future as it has had in the past in preparing pupils for life.

That visit to Nashville made it possible to answer those trying to put pressure on us from outside and also some who were supposed to have the interest of our school at heart.[1]

Oakey Collins (left) and his first cousin Herbert Pershing "Pet" Collins had just finished constructing this model cabin in their manual training class during the 1930s. The cabin, kept all these years, has been donated to the museum by Oakey "Jack" Collins.

True to its word, the state of Tennessee made plans with the Vardy School for an East Tennessee Education Association (ETEA) workshop to be held at Vardy. W. C. Collins recalled, "I remember that the first Greyhound bus I ever saw was while I was at Vardy School. Drew Williams

---

[1]Chester F. Leonard, "Annual Reports," Vardy Community Presbyterian Church Records, 1934.

held me up to the classroom window so . . . I could see the buses and all of the teachers and visitors who were coming for the workshop. School was carried on as usual that day with Mr. Williams demonstrating how audio-visuals could be used in classes to enhance learning. It is still amazing to me that we had all of these wonderful slides, filmstrips, and movies at Vardy during the 30s. We were so far advanced from the other East Tennessee rural schools that people have had a hard time believing my story."[2]

Students were required to participate in regular Bible drills, recitations of selected scriptures. The instructor asked participants to recite memorized verses, including John 3:16.

Explaining the use of slides, Reverend Leonard wrote that Vardy Presbyterian Church and the community elementary school had been using slides for over eleven years. "During that time, we have collected over 4,700 slides that illustrate almost any thought that we wish to make impressive. These slides are on various subjects, including Bible, history, geography, health, citizenship, and agriculture," Leonard noted. However, he did caution that too many slides can defeat the purpose; "but, if the slides fit the thought, too few are seldom shown."[3]

Ruth Jenkins Muhlbauer remembered that "When we were having programs at night when Mr. Leonard would use his slides, he would have us turn on the Delco, which was a little direct current generator. It would run some of the audio-visual equipment. He printed songs on slides so that

---

[2]W. C. Collins, Vardy Oral Histories, personal comments to DruAnna Overbay, 7 August 1996.

[3]Chester F. Leonard, "How We Use Slides," *Church Management* (December 1939).

we could sing them from the screen. When visitors came and made pictures, he would ask them to make slides so that we could see ourselves and community buildings in them. That was really neat because other schools didn't have that kind of thing."[4]

Betty Mullins demonstrates her reading ability to other students as Mr. Leonard supervises. On the front row are Dennis Trent, Kate Mullins, and Beatrice Moore. In the second row are Euna and Beuna Trent, Nelle Ruth Moore, and Alma Mullins. Barbara Mullins is on the back row with Wealthy Moore, Benjamin Moore, and Willie Grohse.

In 1935 not only did the school use slides and filmstrips but also movies were added. Evidently, the school found the right mix of audiovisuals. Over and over in the oral histories, interviewees remembered how effective the slides had been in their instruction. W. C. Collins's comment was typical: "Slides provided us a window to the outside world."[5]

Recalling the slide presentations resulted in alumnus Muhlbauer recollecting that Mr. Leonard also had a good reference library: "He utilized *National Geographic* and had gotten them since 1921 and coded them for use in history classes. He would give us work to do where we would have to use these magazines as reference books to bring back information about different countries to present to our class."[6]

Organization was a key concept. "During the 40s, I guess I didn't think of it in terms of organization, but everything had its time and its place," remembered Billie Mullins Horton.[7] And W. C. Collins recalled, "When we went into the classroom, there were clipboards hanging on the wall which had the subjects that each was studying that day. We would do the assigned

---

[4]Ruth Jenkins Muhlbauer, telephone interviews by DruAnna Overbay, July 2002.

[5]W. C. Collins, Vardy Oral Histories, interviewed by Katie Dorman, Sneedville TN, 7 August 1996.

[6]Muhlbauer.

[7]Billie Mullins Horton, Vardy Oral Histories, interviewed by Katie Doman, Sneedville TN, 9 August 2000.

work and then move on to the next subject. Each student's work was individually planned so we could move at our own pace. As a teacher, many years later, the new educational concept of individual education plans (IEP) was introduced. I thought, That's the way I was taught at Vardy in the 30s. The Vardy program was very progressive and years ahead of its time."[8]

Speaking of the progressive nature of the program, Billie Horton remembered, "Being a teacher, I am constantly aware of new buzzwords such as 'peer tutoring.' No doubt, the staff at Vardy utilized peer tutoring. They didn't call it that at the time, but everybody just kind of worked together."[9]

Stella Miser worked with students in the library, reading to them, listening to them read, and taking them to the manse for Mrs. Leonard's story hour. One of her many goals was to improve oral reading skills.

The best descriptions of Vardy's school curriculum other than the oral histories are through newspaper clippings of student writings about the school activities during the 1940s. Mossie Kate Overton, a Vardy teacher during that period, kept a scrapbook of these clippings, which she gave to the VCHS Museum. Each classroom had a student reporter who wrote about the week's activities. A myriad of voices from the past echo through these writings.

Sarah Mullins noted, "Our school started the first Monday in July with over eighty children. School opens at seven-thirty. We have classes until nine-thirty and then we go upstairs where we have a little lunch. After that we go on the playground, where we play. At ten o'clock the teacher rings the bell; we all go in, get our songbooks, and march into the assembly room. There we have a short program followed by slides. On Monday we have geography slides; Tuesday, health; Wednesday, Bible; and Thursday,

---

[8]W. C. Collins.
[9]Billie Horton.

history. At twelve o'clock we all go back upstairs for lunch; then we play for fifteen minutes. Friday mornings we have classes until lunch. In the afternoon we have activities. . . . "[10]

When Euna and Beuna Trent got a Brownie camera, they brought it to school and let me use it to take this picture. Geraldine Bell (Tootsie Hatfield) gave me this copy when we were doing her oral history of Vardy. Pictured are (front row) Henry Davidson, Dennis Trent, Douglas Williams, Fred Miser, two unidentified students, and Adam Gibson; (second row) Buster Hatfield, Jerry Mullins, Mathis Hatfield, Ruby Roberts, unidentified, Allen Gibson, Ilene Moore, Carolyn Williams, Betty Moore, Ralph Hatfield, Clara Barton, and Phyllis Trent; (third row) Harold Roberts, Kenneth Hatfield, Joe Collins, Harold Williams, Leonard Gibson, Kate Mullins, William Mullins, Charlene Roberts, Troy Williams, Euna Trent, Deanna Moore, Beuna Trent, Beulah Gibson, Anna Belle Barton, and Charles Sexton.

Evidently, one of the highlights of the curriculum was the geography classes. Many of the students wrote about the map-making activities that accompanied their classes. Vardy was a "hands-on" school. Preacher Leonard believed that students learn more and better if they are active participants. Educational studies have proven him correct in this philosophy.

---

[10]Sarah Mullins, *Vardy School Newspaper* article.

"The fifth grade is studying about houses in different parts of the world. . . . D. H. Williams made a pretty map of the British Isles," wrote William Collins.[11]

"We older students are busy making maps of the Vardy Community Center. The one who makes the best map is to have a prize. Some are making splendid maps. Of course, not all of them are good. Jeanette Collins has just finished a map showing domestic animals in Africa. She did a very good job," remarked Jesse Mullins.[12]

George Bells added, "Last week the upper grades made maps of Vardy. Our teacher promised a prize to the one who made the best maps. The prize winners were Josephine Moore, who had the most attractive map, and Cecil Miser for the most exact map."[13]

"Cecil Miser is working on a big map of Italy. . . . Josephine Moore is making a map of Germany," wrote Sarah Mullins.[14]

Esther Mullins included, "We drew a scene of the Sahara Desert in geography."[15]

An entry by Mattie Bell stated, "All of the classes are having a good time drawing maps and coloring them. Later we will put products and things on them."[16]

"The upper grades are studying Africa now," noted Luigene Williams.[17]

"We are still enjoying our map work. Josephine Moore made a map showing the differences in the animals of North and South Africa. Sarah Mullins and Alvin Mullins have been drawing pictures of South Africa," wrote Edward Mullins.[18]

Several times Josephine Moore's name is mentioned with map making, including in this entry by D. H. Williams: "Josephine Moore made a map showing the products of India."[19]

"Edward Mullins and Cecil Miser are making a chart about the contributions of early civilizations. Sarah Mullins and Alvin Mullins made

---

[11]William Collins, *Vardy School Newspaper* article.

[12]Jesse Mullins, *Vardy School Newspaper* article.

[13]George Bell, *Vardy School Newspaper* article.

[14]Sarah Mullins.

[15]Esther Mullins, *Vardy School Newspaper* article.

[16]Mattie Bell, *Vardy School Newspaper* article.

[17]Luigene Williams, *Vardy School Newspaper* article.

[18]Edward Mullins, *Vardy School Newspaper* article.

[19]D. H. Williams, *Vardy School Newspaper* article.

one about the reasons for immigration to this country," wrote Luigene Williams.[20]

Even though geography was stressed, it was not the most important subject taught. Because reading was the most significant, several activities involved this skill. A point of pride was the number of books in each classroom. Mae Williams recalled that "Our room has 114 books which we like to read. We have a reading period in the afternoon. Some of us have read as many as ten."[21]

"We have finished one second reader and are one-fourth the way through another. Our school began in July," noted Betty Mullins.[22]

Margaret Thompson's class included (front row) Euna and Beuna Trent; (second row) Charlene Roberts, Nell Ruth Moore, Betty Mullins, Alma Mullins, Margaret Williams, and Helen Roberts; (third row) Cecil Goins, Wealthy Moore, and Paris Goins; (behind third row) J. B. Goins, Troy Williams, Joe Goins, and James Goins; (back row) Lloyd Williams, R. C. Mullins, and Mack Swiney.

Incorporating art with reading activities seemed to be a big hit with the students since they wrote often about the artwork which accompanied their studies. "The fourth grade has been reading the story 'Sally's Sash.' We

---

[20]Luigene Williams, *Vardy School Newspaper* article.

[21]Mae Williams, *Vardy School Newspaper* article.

[22]Betty Mullins, *Vardy School Newspaper* article.

read how Sally gave her sash to make stars for a flag. We drew pictures of the flag," wrote Edward Mullins.[23]

About another story, Josephine Bell noted, "We read the story 'Moni and the Goats.' Ray Moore and Esther Mullins made a frieze after reading the story. The third graders have been making posters and drawing pictures of the different animals they read about."[24]

"The fifth grade is drawing pictures about Robinson Crusoe's adventures. Some of the history classes are drawing charts about various conquests in history," explained Jean Sizemore.[25]

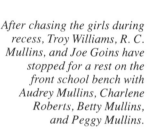
After chasing the girls during recess, Troy Williams, R. C. Mullins, and Joe Goins have stopped for a rest on the front school bench with Audrey Mullins, Charlene Roberts, Betty Mullins, and Peggy Mullins.

"We have been drawing scenes which we read about. One group is drawing pictures about *The Wizard of Oz*. Another group is doing an autumn scene, and a third group did a scene of the Orient," Jesse Mullins wrote.[26]

"We have been drawing pictures on our bulletin board, too. In geography we have made an Eskimo village with people, dogs, and houses," recorded Esther Mullins.[27]

Geraldine Davidson reported, "The boys and I made a picture of Chinese life. We made it out of a large piece of brown wrapping paper. We made Chinese boys and girls, Chinese houses, boats, a pagoda, and a camel's back bridge."[28]

---

[23]Edward Mullins.

[24]Josephine Bell, *Vardy School Newspaper* article.

[25]Jean Sizemore, *Vardy School Newspaper* article.

[26]Jesse Mullins, *Vardy School Newspaper* article.

[27]Esther Mullins, *Vardy School Newspaper* article.

[28]Geraldine Davidson, *Vardy School Newspaper* article.

Dramatic presentations were encouraged via role playing and productions of plays in each classroom. Participating in assembly programs allowed students to develop their speaking skills as well as their self-confidence. "The fourth grade is studying plays in reading. They act out the plays after they read them," recorded W. Collins.[29]

Betty Mullins wrote, "The pupils of the first and second grades have chapel on Friday. We read the Bible lesson, make the announcements, and recite poetry."[30]

The reward system encouraged students to do better. "We have a new rule. In reading, if we do not miss a word, we get a gold star. Some of the class have four stars," noted Willie Jack Gibson.[31]

"We are working hard to see who can get the most gold stars on our reading chart," wrote an unidentified Vardy student.

"Each child who comes every day will get a pencil at the end of this month," reports Charlotte Williams from the second grade while she was a student of Elizabeth Tyler's. Also she reports that the students had been cutting out Mother Goose pictures and that Mrs. Mahan had given their class a picture of a cat.[32]

"We have a graph on our bulletin board showing who is ahead in spelling. The seventh and eighth grade progress is shown with tiny jeeps and the fifth and sixth is shown with Fords. Luigene Williams made the graph; Jean Sizemore made the jeeps and Kenneth Collins made the Fords. Chester Collins is ahead in the higher grades and Bobby Sweeney in the lower," wrote Geraldine Davidson.[33]

Another inscription reads, "The fourth grade have new reading books. Pearl Collins and Esther Mullins got the reading prizes for the second ten weeks. Louise Roberts and Esther Mullins got the spelling prize in our room. Etta Jane Johnson got the writing prize."[34]

Parties, picnics, surprises, and extra goodies were all used as rewards. "We have been having a good time this week. Mrs. Leonard is sponsoring a picnic for the upper grades on Saturday, October 2. We are to bring what we think we can eat, and we will cook our supper outside. The seventh

---

[29]W. Collins.

[30]Barbara Mullins, *Vardy School Newspaper* article.

[31]Willie Jack Gibson, *Vardy School Newspaper* article.

[32]Charlotte Williams, *Vardy School Newspaper* article.

[33]Geraldine Davidson, *Vardy School Newspaper* article.

[34]Esther Mullins and Pearl Collins, *Vardy School Newspaper* articles.

grade wrote invitations as a part of their English work. Edward Mullins, Mae Williams, Josephine Moore and Cecil Miser are planning the games," added Jean Sizemore.[35]

During the school term, the curriculum's schedule changed. In September of that year, Cecil Miser wrote, "We have a new schedule in which we work on one class all day. The next day we study another class. We are having fun. We like it very much because we have time to do all the things we like to do."[36]

Reading these newspaper articles has given VCHS members a better understanding of the curriculum. Since they have been reminded of their school years at Vardy, more windows of their past have been opened. Descriptions of learning tools and methods have convinced them that Vardy was a superior school during its first twenty-five years.

Billie Horton said that "The classes were interactive. Students did primer [kindergarten] and first grade the same year. Usually, if one had readiness skills, that child went on to the first grade. Second grade was also in that one room. When it came time for us to read, we would just turn our little chairs into a circle where we orally read."[37]

Audrey Franz remembered, "About the only reading textbooks that I remember from first grade were the Dick and Jane books. I was so proud when I began reading, 'See Jane. See Jane run.' I don't remember all the stories I read. . . . I will never forget Alyce Williams because she was my first grade teacher and taught me how to read and write."[38]

"There was no child shunned or pushed to the back of the classroom. Every child was worth the teachers' time. They worked with the very slow as well as the academically better students," Billie Horton also recalled.[39]

My brother Dan told me, "There were a lot of hands-on activities. An appreciation of nature was taught. In Father Leonard's workshop, we got to make birdhouses while in science classes we were collecting bird's nests that had been deserted."[40]

---

[35]Jean Sizemore.

[36]Cecil Miser, *Vardy School Newspaper* article.

[37]Billie Horton, interview.

[38]Audrey Mullins Franz, Vardy Oral Histories, interviewed by Katie Doman, Baltimore MD, March 2000.

[39]Billie Horton, Vardy Oral Histories.

[40]Daniel H. Williams, Vardy Oral Histories, interviewed by DruAnna Overbay, Knoxville TN, 15 June 2002.

Class picture 1948–1949.
(Top row) Douglas Williams, Maudie Harris, Geraldine Hatfield, Alyce Williams,
Georgia Mullins, Ollie Fay Johnson, and Dennis Trent; (second row) DruAnna
Williams, Chris Mullins, Henry Davidson (twice), Harold Roberts, and Clarissa Collins;
(third row) Deanna Moore, Roosevelt Mullins, Charles Collins, and Charles L.
Williams; (bottom row) Cecil Goins, Marnie Moore, Robert Moore, Evan Collins,
Perry Dean Goins, Billy Earl Williams, and Maudie Harris.

We went to the museum upstairs to study fossils and rocks. Whenever the focus of our studies changed, so did the museum displays. We were encouraged to touch and get the feel of different objects.

"We had many kinds of learning materials—reading charts on the walls, spiral-bound flip charts on easels, and maps and globes. I didn't realize it at the time that other schools didn't have these materials. I just assumed that they did," recalled Billie Horton.[41]

Troy Williams also enjoyed learning at Vardy: "Flash cards were used to teach us basic math skills. Students would work together to utilize them so that we could quickly associate numbers. There were cards for addition, subtraction, multiplication and division. We had them not only for whole

---

[41]Billie Horton, Vardy Oral Histories.

numbers but for division as well. It was a great method, and it made learning fun."[42]

Billie Horton added that "We also had sentence charts that had different parts of a sentence printed separately. We got to go up front and arrange the different parts to make sentences. We also did a lot of artwork. Each student would get to clip his art onto a string that went around the classroom."[43]

Home Economics classes continued in the school after Mother Leonard's death and through the 1940s. One of the last classes to learn sewing skills until Louise Avery brought the popular program back in the 1960s, included these girls, modeling their circle-tailed skirts. They include Birdie Collins, Alma Mullins, Jeanette Parks, Glessie Collins, Barbara Mullins, Charlotte Williams, Mossie Mullins, Margaret Williams, and Melissa Jane Mullins.

Ruth Jenkins Muhlbauer said, "While the teacher worked with one group, the others would do their homework or work together with the flash cards. That wasn't distracting because there was no unnecessary noise. In fact, the younger ones could learn faster while listening to the teacher work with an older group or while doing the practice work together. . . . Today, I think, they call that cooperative learning. . . . We also changed teachers when subjects changed. . . . If we had social studies or science, we marched into Mr. Leonard's room for that subject. . . . Then another student group would go to another place, learning something else."[44]

---

[42]Troy Williams, Vardy Oral Histories, interviewed by Theresa Burchett, Vardy Church, Sneedville TN, February 2000.

[43]Billie Horton, Vardy Oral Histories.

[44]Muhlbauer, interview.

"The first thing that we did in the morning was go into the assembly room and have prayer and Bible reading," said Charles Sizemore. "It was a religiously themed school."[45]

"Mrs. Leonard taught sewing classes to the seventh and eighth grade girls when I was the seventh grade. In her class, we all made ruffled-tailed skirts. All of the fabric was provided for us, and we did the sewing on treadle sewing machines," wrote my sister Margaret.[46] Margaret also remembered museum trips, slide programs, Bible verse contests, and story time with Mrs. Leonard.

"Every morning we would meet in the auditorium. Students from all of the grades would be together where we would have Bible reading, prayer, and storytelling," R. C. Mullins told me.[47]

This photograph shows Louise Roberts, Bobby Sweeney, and Esther Mullins who have just graduated from the Vardy School.

Mae Sexton also has fond memories from the auditorium. "The auditorium was wonderful because we got to go to concerts held there. Berea College students brought their musical instruments and played for us. They played instruments that we would have never seen at Vardy if they hadn't. They stayed the weekends in various homes while there."[48]

---

[45]Charles Sizemore, interviewed by Theresa Burchett at Vardy Church, Sneedville TN, February 2000.

[46]Margaret Williams Nevels, "Remembering Miss Rankin and Mrs. Leonard," E-mail to DruAnna Overbay, 16 August 2002.

[47]R. C. Mullins, Vardy Oral Histories, interviewed by DruAnna Overbay, Morristown TN, 15 June 2002.

[48]Mae Williams Sexton, Vardy Oral Histories, interviewed by Troy Williams, Laurel MD, 28 September 1999.

Students from the 1950s included (front row) Henry Chris Mullins, Harold
Roberts, Dennis Trent, Paul Gibson, Adam Gibson, Jerry Mullins, and Mack
Arthur Roberts; (second row) Rosa Lee Carroll, Carolyn Williams, Beulah Gibson,
Ruth Roberts, Sally Bea Hatfield, Annabelle Barton, Geraldine (Tootsie) Hatfield,
and Hazel Hoskins; their teacher Drew Williams in in the back with Kate Mullins,
Odell Hoskins, Charles Carroll, Harold Williams, Henry Davidson,
Sherman Carroll, and DruAnna Williams.

Dan Swartz explained, "There was a great emphasis on practical
education and in working with one's hands so the women teachers and the
girls had opportunities to learn how to make things for themselves such as
clothing and do other simple tasks of sewing. They used sewing machines
while the fellows, under Father Leonard, learned how to use the power
tools as well as hand tools. They did a great job with a lathe. It was the first
time I ever saw a lathe at work. Father Leonard was using that so not only
did the children learn how to use tools and operate sewing machines, but
they learned to follow the patterns, which teaches one to follow directions,
a big part of life. Father Leonard allowed others in the community to come
in and use those tools for doing repairs in the church and school as well as

their homes. The shop was a self-contained repair shop as well as a teaching lab."[49]

Reverend Leonard wrote, "Our methods of teaching are improving all the time, continually adapting to the needs of the children of this community."[50] The Berea Extension School of Berea, Kentucky, developed a close relationship with the Vardy School. Having begun the program in 1935, the visiting teachers continued into the 1940s.

Leonard recorded that "For eight sessions the Berea Extension School was held with a total of over 1,280 present. We appreciated the programs furnished by the five [visiting teachers]. . . . Their programs of music, fun, instruction, and worship were well rounded and very helpful to all who attended."[51]

Even though the school did not participate in countywide examinations, Preacher Leonard was not averse to holding his school to high standards by having the students take entrance exams. The rule, which was applied in 1935, was a result of some students' having been expelled, transferring to other county schools, or withdrawing and then returning. Leonard noted in the records, "Any of the people who have been sent from school or had to quit school during former years who would like to come back again to study can take entrance examinations to be enrolled for the new term of school."[52] Later that year several took the examinations, and it was reported that two who had returned after several years' absence, apparently having realized their mistakes, did the best work in the school.

Being able to start school at an early age demanded the same rule. Because I was only five when I entered first grade, Preacher Leonard insisted that I take an entrance exam. It was a readiness test very similar to Peabody's Picture Vocabulary Test. I remember worrying that I would not pass it and thus be unable to go to school; but when I was taking the test, I remember looking up at Mr. Leonard and saying that it was easy.

All who started early had to follow the same guidelines. Those who had taken the entrance exams remembered a similar test. To skip a class, one also had to take an exam to determine if he or she were ready for the next level. Many who had been in the same classroom with other grades

---

[49]Daniel F. Swartz, Vardy Oral Histories, interviewed by DruAnna Overbay, Boone NC, 5 June 1999.

[50]Charles F. Leonard, Vardy Community Presbyterian Church Records.

[51]Leonard, Vardy Community Presbyterian Church Records.

[52]Leonard, Vardy Community Presbyterian Church Records.

remembered listening to advanced lessons when they were supposed to be resting or studying other subjects.

As early as 1930, the school added night classes for adults so that the entire community utilized the school. The night classes were available until the county took over the school. Charles Sizemore recalled: "My father was one who took advantage of those classes. He learned how to work in the blacksmith shop making knives, sickles, and other instruments to aid in cutting."[53]

In many of the annual reports to the church, Preacher Leonard spoke of the adult classes' success. In his 1930 report, he stated: "The night school for adults is my great pride for this year. . . . [N]inety-two took advantage of the program with more than twenty receiving honor certificates. The courses offered during the night school included farm problems, community health, and travel, as well as singing."[54]

Even though the school was put under the public school system in 1944, Preacher Leonard was still in charge of the curriculum. Some of those interviewed felt that the zest and zeal of the curriculum was destroyed once the county assumed the role of curriculum development. Mr. Leonard continued overseeing the work until 1948. Because of his declining health and lack of support from the Presbyterian Board of National Missions, Mr. Leonard left in April of that year to recuperate. He returned for a short time that fall when he realized there was nobody to assume his role. With worsening health problems, he left Vardy in 1952, when I was ten years old.

Expecting that the church would be able to support the school through its efforts, Mr. Leonard wrote Drew Williams, encouraging him to seek funds not only for the school but also for the church, which had no permanent minister. As the church's sessions clerk, Mr. Williams would be corresponding with those specifically mentioned in Leonard's letter: "As part of the Sunday business meeting, I would suggest that a motion of thanks be made and written to Dr. E. O. Kennedy, First Presbyterian Church, Englewood, New Jersey, thanking all of the church for their wonderful friendship and support during these past years."[55]

Others that Mr. Leonard suggested writing were Dr. Lavender of Washington College, Tennessee, to request Presbytery for dissolution of his

---

[53]Charles Sizemore, interview.
[54]Leonard, Vardy Community Presbyterian Church Records, 1930.
[55]Chester F. Leonard, personal correspondence to Drew Williams, 1952.

pastoral relation, and to Dr. Randolph. Leonard's notation in pencil on the letter states, "Rite [*sic*] Randolph Regularly Regarding Replacement."[56]

Several ministers came, but none stayed. The one who was the most frequent during the 1950s was Reverend Charles McKarahan. Others were Raymond Rankin, Dick Nevers, Bob Helm, Edwin White, Calvin A. Duncan, Will Forsythe, G. B. Lewis, Gene Huntzinger, George Mack, Fitzbugh Dotson, C. McCurdy Lipsey, Arnold Johnson, Howard Walton, Bill Diehl, and Brad Spangenburg. Some came only for the summer. The stressed three Rs of the Vardy school which Leonard had transformed from the school's curriculum to the five Rs (Rite Randolph Regularly Regarding Replacement) of getting a minister were not as successful. Today VCHS members have reduced those Rs to one: Remember.

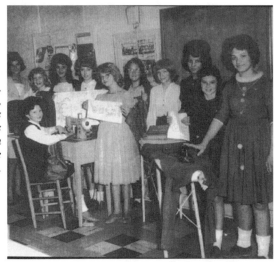

In the 1960s, Frances Mullins, seated at the sewing machine, was one of the students in the sewing class reinstated in the curriculum by Louise Avery and her aide Roxie Davidson.

Others like my dad tried to keep the Vardy School thriving. However, declining attendance reduced the teaching staff to two. After Dad left in 1957, Louise Avery, Presbyterian mission worker, assumed that role. While there, she tried to continue some of the curriculum that had been established at Vardy. Hancock County's lack of proper educational funding led to inadequate maintenance. The deterioration of the schoolhouse and grounds became so bad that the county auctioned it to the Batey Collins

---

[56]Leonard, correspondence.

descendants. Today my brothers, sister, and I own the Vardy School property. Sadly, on October 15, 2003, the Vardy School building, during a windstorm, imploded, and now only a portion of it stands. Undoubtedly, it will need to be completely demolished.

Not only did Vardy families depend on chickens for their eggs, but also kept ducks and geese.

+ + + + +

Making Mud Pies

Mudpies were drying on the
Underground garage roof
Stacked in a single row of ten
One for each of my childhood friends—

Billie Clyde, Georgia Ruth,
Kate, Tootsie, and Sally Bee
Deanna, Black Boy, Dennis,
Harold and Troy Lee.

The white gander goose
Spread his wings, flew to the roof,

Pecked his way through the mud,
Splattering the pies with webbed feet.

Seeing the destruction of my creation,
I donned my Captain Hadachol shirt
And swooped after him from the garage top
Onto the graveled road below.

Sailing on a dream into the mudpuddle,
I awakened to scraped knees,
Hearing my mother's screams,
While the gander pinched my legs blue.

I gathered a fist of mud, flattened it
With a splat, starting all over again
Making mudpies—eleven this time—
Ollie Fay had come to play.

(Remembering 1948 Life in Vardy after the 1996 Vardy School Reunion)

Chapter 13

Staff

Developing the curriculum became one of the minister's goals. Working closely with educators affiliated with the Board of National Missions in New York City as well as long-time friends at Maryville College, Reverend Chester F. Leonard had researched and painstakingly planned his pursuit of a curriculum that prepared students to live a more progressive lifestyle. The first requirement that he instituted was that no teacher could teach at Vardy who did not have a college degree.

Preacher Leonard directed all of the school activities, making sure teachers followed a set curriculum and lesson plans. Shown here on the front steps of the school with him are Betty Mullins and Euna and Beuna Trent, with Beatrice Moore beside him and Dennis Trent in his lap; Mossie Mullins and Beatrice Trent are behind him.

Among the applicants, those with additional course work or a Master's Degree were preferred. This requirement assured that he and Miss Rankin would definitely be on the staff since both had a Master's Degree and that the Board of National Missions would provide another teacher since few in Hancock County fulfilled that requirement. However, it omitted his wife Josephine, as well as three of the community's brightest former students: Eliza Anderson Goins, Stella Miser, and Rosalie Mullins. By instituting a plan for teacher aides, however, he was able to hire them, provided they were involved in a continuing education plan. Wishing to give students practical learning experiences, he included vocational classes, the first taught in Tennessee. Realizing he needed to utilize the talents of both of his parents to teach and develop this phase of the program, he persuaded them to join the staff by presenting them the option of living in the school and remaining close to their son or continuing to live in Birmingham.

An agreement between the county and the Presbyterian Board of National Missions stipulated that the school would be considered a county school and furnish one teacher there, but all other aspects such as curriculum, maintenance, and additional teachers would be the Presbyterians' responsibility. The Board of National Missions, whose emissary was Reverend Chester F. Leonard, would tolerate no interference of any sort.[1] For the county it was a "sweetheart deal." They felt relief that they would not have the expense of building a school at Vardy since the Presbyterians had already done so twice on private property.

Rosalie Mullins and Stella Miser were two former Vardy students that Mr. Leonard would ask to work as aides in the school while they pursued their education. Rosalie, however, did not work long, as she met and married her husband at Berea.

During the first two years, the three teachers at Vardy included not only the minister and Miss Rankin but also Mildred Renegar, who was later replaced by Helen Gleason. Renegar and Gleason were both considered Board of National Missions teachers. Miss Rankin, having been considered a county teacher before, was the Hancock County School Board's appointee. Stella Miser and Rosalie Mullins assisted Miss Rankin by working in the preschool program in the basement of the school. They were sent to Berea College for their continuing course work when Vardy School was not in session.

Muhlbauer explained, "My Aunt Stella, she was a teacher too. She went away to school, and then she came back and helped with the younger kids. . . . Later on she went to Berea during summer months to earn college

---

[1]Vardy Community Presbyterian Church Records.

credits."[2] Eliza Goins assisted Mother Leonard in the home economics classes.

"Stella Miser worked with the younger ones on the ground floor; Miss Rankin taught first, second, and third on the second floor; Miss Gleason taught grades three-A and fourth while Mr. Leonard taught fifth, sixth, seventh, and eighth," Cleland Collins told me.[3] Others who were interviewed said that Mrs. John (Sally) Burrows taught four-A and fifth. Church records refer to both Mrs. Burrows and Miss Gleason. Whether or not Burrows and Gleason were different women or the same one who later was married remains unclear. At times, it seems the names were used synonymously and at other times to indicate different individuals. One of those interviewed, however, claimed, "Miss Gleason's first name was 'Helen,' so they had to have been two different people."[4] These two names were located on the visiting teachers list as occupants of the visiting teachers' quarters of the school.

Assuming roles as teachers as well as maintenance directors, the minister's parents, referred to as Mother and Father Leonard, lived in an apartment on the school's top floor.

Even though Mr. Leonard and Miss Gleason were responsible for students in specific grade levels, they shared the same students since the older grade levels were departmentalized and grouped. Grouped according

---

[2]Ruth Jenkins Muhlbauer, telephone interviews by DruAnna Overbay, July 2002.

[3]Cleland Collins, Vardy Oral Histories, interviewed by Sally Collins and DruAnna Overbay, Morristown TN, 25 April 1999.

[4]Oakey Collins, telephone interview by DruAnna Overbay, June 2003.

to abilities, each was able to develop basic skills and yet be challenged if possessing greater abilities.

One teacher other than Mr. Leonard who repeatedly is referred to on the oral-history tapes is my dad, Drew B. Williams. Dad joined the staff in 1931, replacing Miss Gleason.

From 1931 to 1942, Dad taught at Vardy. Mom began teaching there in 1944 and continued until 1955. Dad returned in 1950, after having served as superintendent and as principal of Hancock County High School and Alanthus Hill Elementary School. He remained at Vardy until 1957 when we moved to Knoxville, where both my parents continued their teaching careers.

The 1931 annual report to the community reflects the success that the new school's staff was experiencing. Reverend Leonard reported: "Miss Rankin has a smaller group with which to work. She can give more attention to each child and help it get started in the right way. Stella Miser assists during part of the morning, taking the small groups to the room downstairs where she can carry on a definite program for them. . . . Mr. Williams is doing good work in his room and on the playground. Because of his faithfulness and willingness to try what is asked of him, I count this as the easiest year that I have had as leader in this schoolwork. Mrs. Leonard is getting better results in reading than she did last year. The boys working with Father are putting improvements on the grounds and doing what they can to learn how to best take care of property. The homemaking classes are also doing beautiful work. . . . For the first time, I am able to give individual instruction in my room. My pupils are meeting me nicely with their fine interest, cooperation, and willingness to try."[5]

---

[5]Chester F. Leonard, Vardy Community Annual Report, Vardy Community Presbyterian Church Records, 1931.

W. C. Collins told Doman, "There were approximately 125 students in attendance at Vardy when I went to school. There were seven teachers on the staff. The minister taught as well as his wife, mother, and father."[6]

"Mr. Williams was one of my teachers," explained Muhlbauer. "He taught so much in the fourth grade, including spelling, reading, arithmetic, and history. Mr. Leonard taught world history, social studies, and other similar subjects. . . . Fourth, fifth, and sixth [grades] were in Drew's room, and then seventh, eighth, and eight-B were in Mr. Leonard's room. For most of our classes, we had different teachers."[7]

During 1931–1935, the core teaching staff was Mary J. Rankin, Drew Williams, and Chester F. Leonard. Helen Stewart joined the staff in 1935, making four full teachers other than the minister's parents and wife. Helen was replaced by Ianella F. Rhea for the 1936–1937 year.

Mossie Kate Overton,
who lived at Mulberry Gap,
lived in the visiting teacher quarters
and in the Rankin Mission House
while she taught at Vardy Community School.

Having finished eight years at Vardy School, W. C. (Claude) Collins was one of two students honored during commencement exercises at the Vardy Presbyterian Church on Wednesday, March 10, 1943. "A very interesting program was presented. Short talks were made by each of the teachers as they presented grades to their students. Rev. C. F. Leonard, Mrs. Sally (John) Burrows, Miss Stella Miser, and Miss Mary J. Rankin told of the work that had been done during the year. Superintendent Drew B. Williams presented the diplomas to the graduates, Claude Collins and Ralph Goins," wrote W. P. Grohse.[8]

---

[6]W. C. Collins, Vardy Oral Histories, interview by Katie Doman, 7 August 1996.

[7]Muhlbauer, telephone interviews by DruAnna Overbay, July 2002.

[8]W. P. Grohse, Vardy Community Presbyterian Church Records, 1943.

Speaking often about the influence his Vardy teachers have had on his life, Claude Collins said that he looked to Drew Williams and Preacher Leonard as his male role models. "Drew always dressed nicely and was friendly to everyone, and I have always tried to follow his example. Being in charge of the school, Preacher Leonard used slides, filmstrips, and movies to accompany the lesson plans. When we finished the eighth grade, we were sent to Warren Wilson in North Carolina or Berea in Kentucky to attend high school," Collins said.[9]

Margaret Thompson began teaching at Vardy in 1946. She became a registered nurse and has remained lifelong friends with Miss Horton.

Elizabeth Horton began teaching at Vardy after her high school graduation in 1946. She returned to school and got her degree in registered nursing. She married "Mutt" Davidson.

Ruth Jenkins Muhlbauer remembered, "Now the county provided one additional teacher at Vardy. Mr. Williams was hired as a county employee. I think he got $30 per month from the county and an additional five dollars from the Presbyterian Board."[10] Miss Rankin continued as a county employee.

When my father [Drew Williams] was elected Hancock County school superintendent in 1942, Sally Burrows assumed his position at the school for that year. Dad was superintendent until 1948. Mr. Leonard and Miss Rankin continued teaching in the school.

After my father assumed leadership of the county schools, he recommended to the Hancock County school board that the county pay for three teachers for the 1943–1944 school year. The new teachers still had to be college graduates. Agreeing to Dad's proposal, the board filled the positions by hiring Mossie Kate Overton as principal, Lois Mahan, and

---

[9]W. C. Collins, Vardy Oral Histories, personal comments to DruAnna Overbay, 7 August 1996.

[10]Ruth Jenkins Muhlbauer, telephone interviews by DruAnna Overbay, July 2002.

Elizabeth Tyler. Mr. Leonard became the director of the school as well as continuing to teach. Principal Overton remembered, "The year before I went to Vardy, Mr. and Mrs. Leonard came into my class at Sunnyside, where I was teaching. 'Do you mind if we visit your classroom?' Mr. Leonard asked. When I said, 'Come on in,' they sat for maybe an hour while I went right on with my teaching. They left after having said, 'Thank you.' That's all they said. I never heard from them again until that summer when Mr. Williams came and asked me if I would be principal at Vardy. Being young, I was anxious to leave home so I agreed since I would live away from home. I stayed in the visiting teachers' quarters and in Miss Rankin's cottage when she went to Florida for the cold months. I don't think the Leonards knew I wasn't a college graduate, so you see, that visit to my classroom in Sunnyside was sort of like an interview, I guess.

"Now, I only had a two-year teaching certificate, so I just kept quiet because Drew told me to."[11]

Unable to fill all the positions with college graduates, Dad did not inform either Mr. Leonard or the Board of National Missions of this fact.

The articles written by students during Miss Overton's tenure at Vardy were cited in the previous chapter.

My sister Margaret wrote, "Miss Elizabeth Tyler was my primary/first grade teacher. Going to school in first grade was exciting because she taught me how to count and read. I not only learned from her but also by listening to her as she taught other children in the classroom, especially the second grade.

"Stella Miser helped Miss Tyler with our classes by leading us to the library, where she was the librarian, and helping us choose library books. She also would stay with us during rest time, a time after lunch and recess when we would have a chance to relax and become quiet before we started our afternoon classes. Stella was not only my teacher but became a lifetime friend. We corresponded regularly up until her death."[12]

While Mossie Kate Overton was principal, she encouraged students to write by submitting articles to the newspaper for publication and corresponding with Vardy soldiers who were fighting in World War II.

---

[11]Mossie Kate Overton Campbell, telephone interview by DruAnna Overbay, June 2003.

[12]Margaret Nevels, "Remembering Vardy," manuscript given to DruAnna Overbay, 12 July 2000.

During the summer of 1944, both Lois Mahan and Elizabeth Tyler left Vardy. Lois Mahan moved to Knoxville, where she resumed her teaching career in the Karns Community. Even though those interviewed were unsure whether Miss Tyler had moved to another position or had died that summer or later, they did remember that she tragically lost her life by drowning while vacationing near the ocean.

The fall of 1944 through 1945 brought Ruth Livesay and my mother Alyce Williams as Mahan's and Tyler's replacements. Mom was one of the first teachers that the Board of National Missions allowed to teach there without a college degree. She had been teaching in other area schools such as Coleman's, Hall's, Yellow Branch, and Sycamore. Based on a two-years-of-college certificate and her teaching experience, the Board of National Missions permitted her to teach at Vardy Community School.

Helen Stewart Mullins, one of the first Vardy
students to graduate from college,
got her degree from Maryville College,
a Presbyterian-affiliated school.
She began her teaching career
and principalship at Vardy
in 1947 and continued through 1950.

Audrey Mullins Franz told me, "When I started at Vardy, Alyce Williams was my teacher. I'll never forget Alyce. She had such a hard time trying to get me to write on the lines of my paper. Instead of writing on the lines, I would begin on one line and end up three or four lines on down the paper. . . . She kept saying, 'Audrey, I don't know what else to do with you,' but she kept right on working with me until I finally learned how to write on a straight line. That's the one thing I'll always remember about Alyce Williams."[13]

---

[13]Audrey Mullins Franz, Vardy Oral Histories, interviewed by Katie Doman, Baltimore MD, March 2000.

And Leonard Gibson noted that "My first teacher was Alyce Williams. I remember how nice she was to everyone. She had a goal in mind for us; she wanted every student to get an education. Everyone just loved her."[14]

When school began in the fall of 1945, the new principal Elmer Turner and Flora Church joined Alyce Williams. Of course, Mr. Leonard continued as the director. After one year at Vardy, Mr. Turner and Miss Church were placed in other schools.

Several students of the 1940s and early 1950s remembered specific teachers and incidents of their classroom days. My sister Margaret is one: "My mother Alyce Williams was my second grade teacher. My only spanking at school came from my mother. She had assigned the second graders to write a story. While we were working, she asked specifically that there be no talking. Some of the children continued to talk. Then she told us that if she heard any of us talking she would have to spank us. The boy next to me, Pete Sweeney, asked me a question, and I answered him. Mother then told Pete and me to come up for our spankings. Pete went up, and he held out his hand while she spanked it with a ruler. Then it was my turn. I didn't go up when she called me. The second time she called me, I stood up and ran in the opposite direction. Yes, I did also get that hand spanking at school. Then that evening when my mother told my dad about the event, I received another spanking at home because I had run from my mother. I learned my lesson!"[15]

Even though World War II had ended, the shortage of college graduates entering the field of education became critical. So many were pursuing degrees which would allow them to enter the medical field or other careers that would be beneficial to the military in the event of another war.

As a result, high school graduates were permitted to teach at Vardy School. Mr. Leonard asked my father, Drew Williams, to secure the brightest and best Hancock County High School graduates.

David Swartz wrote: "My first experience with Vardy School was going with your father [Mr. Williams] in June or July to Mulberry Gap to look for a teacher because they needed someone for the other grades. Mr. Leonard had not been teaching on a full-time basis nor was Mr. Williams since he was the county school superintendent. So I went with him to Mulberry Gap and then to Sneedville to interview two young ladies. They

---

[14]Leonard Gibson, "Remembering Vardy School," manuscript given to interviewer Katie Doman, Baltimore MD, 6 March 2000.

[15]Nevels, "Remembering Vardy."

both accepted that afternoon. . . . They were Elizabeth Horton and Margaret Thompson. They were there for the 1946-47 school year . . . and these two were intelligent young people . . . good teachers as far as I know, but they had no formal training beyond high school."[16]

In May 2002, Macie Mullins received a letter from Elizabeth Horton Davidson describing that year at Vardy. The following are excerpts from that letter.

"I planned to go to nursing school in the fall of 1946; however, those plans changed slightly. On a Sunday afternoon before I was supposed to start nursing school, Mr. Williams came by and asked me if I would consider teaching at Vardy School that school year. I thought about it and decided that I would like to try this for the school year.

"I spent the school year at Vardy meeting many lovely people, spending much time with my dear friend Margaret Thompson, and getting to know Alyce Horton Williams. These two dear ladies were a joy to work with. Reverend and Mrs. Leonard and Dave Swartz were also a pleasure to work with, and so much help. I was fortunate to be able to board at the home of Bill and Lillian Grohse. God had never created nicer or more hospitable people than they. Aunt Nancy Miser, Lillian's mother, lived next door. Every evening Lillian and I went to visit her. . . .

"I owe so much to each of my students that year. Each of them helped add a new dimension to my life. I started out being the shyest person who ever attempted to be a teacher. It wasn't long before the shyness began to evaporate. I developed self-confidence, thanks to my pupils, that I would never have had otherwise. . . . "[17]

Margaret Nevels recalled that "Miss Margaret Thompson was my third and fourth grade teacher. Miss Thompson was just about the neatest teacher I had ever seen. She was young, pretty, and thoughtful. Her mother made her many dresses, and each day she would come to school wearing a beautiful dress, starched and neatly ironed. She was a model to all of us girls."[18]

Leonard Gibson said, "When it was time to move up to the third grade, we had Miss Margaret Thompson. She was very nice but a little stricter

---

[16]David F. Swartz, "They Came. They Stayed," manuscript given to Vardy Community Historical Society, June 2001.

[17]Elizabeth Horton Davidson, letter to Macie Mullins, May 2002.

[18]Nevels, "Remembering Vardy."

than my first teacher. Grades three, four, and five all met in her room. The teachers all did a great job, and they were willing to help at any time."[19]

And Troy Williams remembered that "All of the boys in the school were in love with Miss Thompson. She got our attention and kept it because we wanted to impress her. . . . She was a great teacher, too and because she was so pretty, we couldn't help but pay attention to her teaching."[20]

In 1947 Helen Stewart, who married Frank Mullins, moved back into the community. During the war years, Frank had been working in Oak Ridge, where they had lived, but since they both wanted to return home, they bought a place on Newman's Ridge. Helen Stewart Mullins was appointed principal of Vardy that year. She remained in that position until the fall of 1951, when Drew Williams returned as principal and she became a teacher.

John Mullins visits with Drew Williams, who had been his teacher when he was a student at Vardy. They had developed a friendship beyond that of teacher and student. This would be the last time they would see each other.

"We had so many wonderful teachers at Vardy. One who I will always remember is Helen Mullins. She was kind, patient, gentle, and always a lady," wrote Glessie Collins Cummins.[21]

Teachers with Mrs. Mullins during 1947 were Orpha Johnson and Alyce Williams. In 1948 Margaret Thompson returned for one year, having

---

[19]Leonard Gibson, interview.

[20]Troy Williams, Vardy Oral Histories, interviewed by Theresa Burchett, Vardy Church Sneedville TN, March and April 2000.

[21]Glessie Collins Cummins. Vardy School Alumni Questionnaire. 4 September 2004.

finished one year of nurse training. She replaced Orpha Johnson. Returning to school the next fall, Miss Thompson was replaced by Louise Rhea.

In 1951 after Mrs. Mullins was appointed principal of another school, she left Vardy. Hoye Brown replaced her. Because of a drop in enrollment, Vardy had only two teachers during the remaining years of the school. My parents Drew and Alyce Williams both taught there until 1955. That year, my mother, Alyce Williams, was placed at Elm Springs. Mossy Mullins, another Vardy student and Hancock County High School graduate, replaced her. In the fall of 1956, Mom returned to Vardy. The following year our family moved to Knoxville. Mom taught first grade at Powell, Norwood, and Pleasant Ridge, where she remained until her retirement. Dad was principal at Hieskell, Ridgewood, and West Haven Elementary Schools. He continued in his position until he was seventy.

As enrollment fell, continuing school at Vardy under only two teachers was a struggle. Those teaching after my parents were Louise Avery, Deanna Cody, Elmer Turner, and Arnold Johnson, who replaced Elmer Turner. Roxie Davidson, a former Vardy student, was an aide during this time period. Louise Avery, a Presbyterian missionary, lived in the Chester F. Leonard manse and continued the church work. However, she was placed at Kyle's Ford Elementary School in 1971. During that year Bill Phillips and Arnold Johnson taught at Vardy. When Vardy School became a one teacher school in 1972, Carolyn Rasnic was the teacher. Then during 1973–1974, Christine Penelton was Vardy's last full-time teacher.

When the schoolhouse was no longer safe for use, the county brought in a portable classroom. A Head-Start program was housed there, supervised by Mae Williams Sexton. Eventually, during the 1970s, the school was closed.

A special treat for me was to go to work with Daddy when he was superintendent of Hancock County, and to visit the high school.

+ + + + +

Daddy

Life was never simple for you, was it?
Born a coal miner's son
Studying Latin's every discipline
Teaching called you, claimed you,
Keeping the writer hidden within.

You read to us every night or recited some bit of poetry
You memorized in school
"Rapunzle, Rapunzle, let down your golden hair,"
You'd laugh and run your fingers through my hair
Or sit me on the porch bannister
Pointing to the moon crawling over Newman's Ridge,
"I see the moon and the moon sees me
God bless the moon
And God bless DruAnnie."

"Wear a baby blue dress,"
You would say
And slip me an extra dollar or two
Even when I was making money on my own.

Life was never simple to you
But it made you the gentleman
It was "please and thank you"
Even when I gave you a last sip of water
You opened your eyes,
Smiled, whispered,
"Thank You,"
As you clutched my hand.

Daddy,
I wore a baby blue dress
Just for you.

(After Daddy's death, 21 July 1998)

Chapter 14
Vardy Community Presbyterian Center

My sister Margaret Nevels noted that "Vardy Community Presbyterian Center was truly a community for all who lived there in the 1940s and 1950s when I was growing up. We had church and school, as well as activities such as dinners, movies, game night, baseball games, and special music programs provided by Berea College and Warren Wilson College."[1]

David Swartz said, "It is hard to separate the church from the school and community because they were the same. That is why it was called Vardy Community Center. Even though some were active members in the Presbyterian Church, they were also active in other churches in the evening."[2]

Community leaders often met with other residents at the school to have dinner on the grounds, promoting community spirit and unity.

The community center included not only the buildings and the cluster of activities that were held there but also community leaders, who included the church ministers, missionaries, church elders, and members. During the first years of the church, Noah Collins and Elkana (Caney) Collins were the

---

[1]Margaret Williams Nevels, "Remembering Vardy," manuscript given to DruAnna Overbay, 12 July 2000.

[2]David F. Swartz, Vardy Oral Histories, interviewed by DruAnna Overbay, Boone NC, 5 June 1999.

elders. In November 1922, Clay Miser replaced Noah Collins as elder after Noah's death. Other church and community leaders who were singled out for praise were ushers Ed Williams and Barlow Collins, as well as the financial committee consisting of Daniel B. Horton, Frank Miser, and Mrs. Rhea (Eliza) Saddler. Logan and Nancy Miser, Mae Miser, and Herbert Collins were often mentioned as helpers during the early 1920s. Elders elected in November 1927 were Brownlow Mullins and Frank Miser. The church records report that the Thanksgiving address on November 29, 1928, was given by Steve Gibson, a member of the church. Others mentioned as leaders of the community were Mrs. Docia Miser and Burkett Mullins. Adding to the list of influential leaders during the late 1920s were Lloyd Sizemore, Marshall Davidson, Mr, and Mrs. Hughie Mullins, and Mrs. Brownlow Mullins.

After laying rock for a new sidewalk to the church, residents of the community gathered for a group celebration, which included a variety of desserts prepared by the ladies.

On February 19, 1933, other community leaders to rejoin the church were Lillian Grohse and Alyce Williams, who had moved their letters when they left the state. Joining the church were Drew B. Williams, William (Bill) Grohse, Darnell Williams, Eliza Williams, Belva Williams and Cynthia Williams. Drew and Bill were elected elders in October, 1938. In April 1939 several members who joined the church and emerged as church and community leaders included William P. Grohse, Sr., Amos Gibson, Anderson Bell, Alice Gibson, Callie Bell, and William H. Leonard. Anderson Bell was elected as an elder the following October.

During a sessions meeting in December 1939, Frank Miser noted that "Plans were discussed for small group meetings after the first of the year to do definite work for the betterment of the homes, community, and church."[3] Committees were formed to work together for community improvement. The chairpersons included Anderson Bell, playground; Pauline Moore, lunchroom: Mrs. Leonard, health and leadership; William P. Grohse, Jr., Bible reading; Reverend C. F. Leonard, conservation; Cynthia Williams, road; Dinah Mullins, plays; and Julia Sizemore, choir.

Community and church leaders often met to plan and discuss activities for Saturday and Sunday afternoons. During the 1930s, they included William "Father" Leonard, Josephine Leonard, Asa "Pa" Gibson, Frank Miser, Docia Miser, and Dora Williams. On the second row are Drew Williams, Preacher Leonard, Edward Williams, Marshall Davidson, Edward Miser, and Carson Mullins. The back row leaders are Alyce Williams, Louis Collins, Bertha Collins, Albert Mullins, Ernest Miser, Coby Gibson, Gilbert Gibson, Logan Miser, and Herbie Collins.

"The church and school personnel were interested in trying to provide a well-rounded education including spiritual, mental, and physical well-being," wrote Nevels.[4]

These individuals were actively involved in planning community activities. According to James D. Martin, "Certain nights are set aside for

---

[3]Frank Miser, Vardy Community Presbyterian Church Records, 1939.
[4]Nevels, "Remembering Vardy."

meetings for people of all ages. . . . They play games, sing, listen to records of the best music, see moving pictures, and have a question-and-answer period on farm, home, and problems of the day."[5]

The Burkett Mullins family was involved in many of the community activities, since several of his children were Vardy students. Many of his descendents are actively involved in the VCHS.

Children of the 1940s remember well these activities that the leaders of the community had initiated. "To promote community activity and family togetherness, the church/school had potluck dinners. During the summer these were held on the picnic grounds above the school. In the winter they were held in the school lunchroom. Mother would usually bake all day in preparation. Her specialties were lemon meringue pies and Southern fried chicken which she would take," Nevels noted.[6]

"My mommy baked fruitcakes, sweetcakes, pies, and all kinds of desserts to take to the dinners," Audrey Mullins Franz told Doman.[7] The dinners were much anticipated events because many women looked forward to "showing off" their best recipes. Pickles, relishes, jams, and jellies adorned the tables with other favorite foods, including corn, beans, sweet potatoes, deviled eggs, and potato salad.

Robert Moore told me, "One of the things that we looked forward to was going to movies at Vardy. That is where we got acquainted with Roy Rogers, Trigger, Dale Evans, and Gabby Hayes. Cowboy movies were our

---

[5]James D. Martin, "McCormick Alumnus: C. F. Leonard," *McCormick Speaking* (November 1947).

[6]Nevels, "Remembering Vardy."

[7]Audrey Mullins Franz, Vardy Oral Histories, interviewed by Katie Doman, Baltimore MD, March 2000.

favorite. Hopalong Cassidy, Gene Autry, Buster Crabbe, and whoever was starring in the movies became our favorite cowboys. That was one of the few pleasures we had. When Mr. Williams had to change the spool or movie reel, we would sit there praying that the second part of the movie had been sent so we'd get to see the rest of it. Sometimes we were sent movies in serials of one episode at a time that carried to another episode."[8]

In the fall of 1925, Herbie Collins and Lewis Johnson repair the walkway. The young boys observing are Walter and Edward Miser. At the saw is Preacher Leonard. Behind the saw are Grover Mullins, Frank Miser, and Clay Miser. Holding the log are two young boys, Jasper Mullins and Joe Dan Stewart. James Stewart is helping the preacher saw.

"On game nights the adults would teach the children new games. Herbie Collins was so gentle and patient teaching us how to play checkers. We had dominoes, Pick-up Stix [or Jack Straws], and other board games," noted Nevels.[9] "We also had music programs and could count on there being plays for the holidays," added Billie Horton.[10]

Community Workings

The community's closeness to its church and school was enhanced by community meetings and workings. The local news reported weekly about the activities in which the community members were involved. In a school news article, Mossie Kate Overton noted, "We held another 'wood

---

[8]Robert Moore, Vardy Oral Histories, interviewed by DruAnna Overbay, Talbott TN, 13 July 2002.

[9]Nevels, "Remembering Vardy."

[10]Billie Mullins Horton. Vardy Oral Histories, interviewed by Katie Doman, Sneedville TN, 9 August 2000.

working' on Thursday, November 11. Among those present were George Johnson, Carson Moore, Donald Bell, Herbert Collins, W. P. Grohse, Jr., Anderson Bell, Tiny Lee Mullins, Darnell Williams, Gilbert Gibson, Asa Gibson, Alfred Mullins, W. H. Leonard, and our preacher, Rev. C. F. Leonard. Several who couldn't attend the 'working' have promised to deliver wood to the school. These include Squire B. M. Mullins, Albert Mullins, and Worley Davidson."[11]

After a laborious morning cutting timber, these men take a break before hauling the timber to the school and church. The timber would be cut for use not only in those buildings but also in the Rankin cottage and the manse.

"The money which would have been used to buy wood for the school has been matched by the state and will be used to buy reading books for the school library," added Mattie Bell.[12] Newer books were considered a luxury. Community workings also provided much-needed money for other supplies since funds were scarce for scissors, crayons, construction paper, and glue for art projects.

Bell had recognized at an early age that the community in which she lived was unique. She wrote in a school report, "We feel sure there is no other community where parents bring nicer surprises to their school. As boys and girls of Vardy School, we want to thank them."

In addition to the wood-gathering activities, the workings included maintenance work. "Mr. Leonard and Father Leonard have put a new roof on the church. They are now mending the schoolhouse roof," Bell added.[13] Community members dropped by to help with the roofing as they learned that the work was being done.

Community workings were common during the 1920s, 1930s, and 1940s. "I remember we had wood cutting or work days to provide wood for

---

[11]Mossie Kate Overton, *Vardy School News*, 1943.

[12]Mattie Bell, *Vardy School Newspaper* article.

[13]Mattie Bell, *Vardy School Newspaper* article.

heating both the school and the church. That was all the fuel we had. The women, of course, brought basket lunches for the men who cut the wood," Cleland Collins informed me.[14]

Aunt Lizzie Collins, my grandfather Horton's sister, is shown here with four of her sons— Joe Dan Stewart standing beside her, Boyd Collins in her lap, and Herbert Pershing Collins and Carlos Stewart Collins.. She was one of the cooks in the school lunchroom during the 1930s and 1940s.

Hot Lunch Program

Community involvement was necessary in many of the school's activities, especially the hot-lunch program. Being one of the first rural schools in Tennessee to provide hot lunches for the children, much was dependent on community support. Church records indicate that during the Thanksgiving service on November 28, 1929, the school's lunchroom was utilized by the church. The dinner at the school was attended by more than 200 people. Those in the community brought covered dishes to share. During the service, the minister asked for donations for the lunch program, which resulted in donations of $39.87 as well as produce.

Throughout the years, the community's willingness to participate is recorded. The 1943 church record states: "Mrs. C. F. Leonard gave a report of the financial aid given by the people of the church and community. The total receipts were $392.70 plus canned goods and supplies which were given. The following were given: 88 quarts of apples, 34 quarts of tomatoes, 53 quarts of beans, 1 quart of corn, 9 quarts of peaches, 7 quarts of relish, 12 quarts of pears, 29 quarts of berries, 5 quarts of pepper, 2 quarts of rhubarb, for a total of 240 quarts."

---

[14]Cleland Collins, interview.

My father noted in the church records, "The following were also given: half bushel of beans, three and a quarter bushels of potatoes, two bushels of pears, half bushel of sweet potatoes, one pound of butter, three gallons of milk, and 24 pounds of crackers. Mr. Leonard thanked all for their active support of the hot lunches and told of the good they were doing the school children."[15]

Often, women in the community worked together to provide for other food needs. "Mrs. Nancy Miser, Mrs. Lillian Grohse, Mrs. Florence Williams, Mrs. Alyce Williams, and Mrs. Mary Grohse spent Wednesday in Sneedville canning carrots for school lunch. They filled 108 quarts," Principal Overton reported.[16]

Emily Gibson and her sister Pauline Gibson Moore are shown in this picture. Pauline was one of the cooks at Vardy, sharing the job with Stella Miser.

Not only did the lunchroom provide hot lunches for the children but it also was the place to teach proper dining etiquette. Teachers encouraged children to use "Please" and "Thank you" often, as well as taught them how to set a proper table. Polite conversation was allowed as long as children correctly used their knives and forks. "Mrs. Goins has the dining room decorated. Each table has a bunch of Christmas flowers or a little Christmas tree on it. The table which showed the most manners got little Santas on it," reported D. H. Williams.[17]

Robert Moore recalled: "My mother, Pauline Gibson Moore, was a cook at Vardy for several years. It always amazed me what Mother and the

---

[15]Drew B. Williams, Vardy Community Presbyterian Church Records, 1943.

[16]Mossie Kate Overton (Campbell), telephone interview.

[17]D. H. Williams, *Vardy School Newspaper* article.

other ladies could do with so little. . . . I remember especially the ladies who cooked there. It was such a pleasure when we sat down to eat dinner. I guess they call it lunch now, but back in our day, it was dinner and supper. At dinnertime we always got a good meal. (It seems that most often it was beans and cornbread.)"[18]

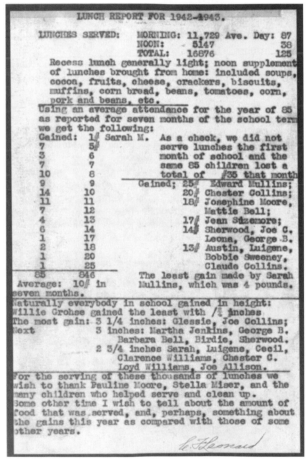

The "Lunch Report for 1942–1943" shows the meticulous record keeping of Reverend Leonard in his never-ending attempt to thwart malnutrition.

Not all of those interviewed remembered eating lunch in the lunch-room. "I took my lunch, but there were some who were less fortunate than I, and the school would provide lunch for them," Charles Sizemore said.[19]

---

[18]Robert Moore, interview.

[19]Sizemore, interview.

"My brother and I didn't have to pay for our lunches because after lunch or before lunch sometimes we would get to go up to the lunchroom and set tables up and after lunch we'd close the tables. As a result, we ate lunch free," R. C. Mullins said. "Sometimes we washed the dishes and took out the trash. At other times we would sweep the floor. I don't remember who else helped do these jobs, but I know I did for my lunch. We also raked a ton of leaves off the walks outside the school."[20]

Little Alice Williams, one of the cooks during the 1950s, attended her granddaughter's wedding at Vardy in the 1970s. Leaving the church with her is Vardy Collins, the son of Noah Collins, the church's first clerk.

One of the last cooks to serve at Vardy was Willa Mae Mullins, shown here with her son Jack, one of the charter board members who is very active with the VCHS.

Lloyd Williams recalled that "Even those who had no money to buy the hot lunches every day were not left out. The parents took care of that. If one was too poor to give money, then the parents raised enough vegetables during the summer and canned them. When one of the church members came around and asked each family what they could do to help, my mother always donated 40 or 50 cans."[21]

---

[20]R. C. Mullins, interview.
[21]Lloyd Williams, interview.

Glessie Collins Cummins wrote, "We were the poorest dressed at Vardy and had less food than anyone at school. One of my fondest memories of going to school there was eating the hot lunch. It was the only balanced meal we had each day."[22]

And Thomas Collins said, "When I was going to school, I'd try to sneak upstairs to help in the lunchroom, set the table or whatever needed to be done. I always got a little extra food that way. I enjoyed helping in the lunchroom."[23]

I remember several different ladies who cooked at school when I was there. Aunt Lizzie Collins, Eliza Goins, Pauline Moore, and 'Lit-Mammy' Williams were the ones I remember most because they always had some sort of dessert. My favorite was the candy they made from powdered sugar mixed with Pet canned cream, peanut butter, and corn flakes.

Stella Miser was cook when Audrey Mullins Franz went to school. She remembered Stella's asking her to go to her mother's turnip patch and pick a big bag of turnip greens for the school lunches. Audrey Franz remembered, "Stella would say, 'Audrey, I'd like to have some mustard greens,' and I would go into the field and pick mustard and turnip greens to take to her. She would pay me a quarter for them. She cooked for us all the time, and I would get to work in the kitchen for my lunches and save my money to buy something at Bill Grohse's store."[24]

"Before I began cooking at Vardy, my mother Julie Collingsworth Gibson was the cook. She cooked there while Alyce and Drew were the teachers in the early 50s,"[25] recalled Willa Mae "Blue Eyes" Mullins, who began cooking for Vardy students during the years that Louise Avery taught.

---

[22]Glessie Collins Cummings, Vardy Community School Questionnaire, 4 September 2004.

[23]Thomas Collins, Vardy Oral Histories, interviewed by Sally Collins, West Liberty KY, June 21, 2002.

[24]Audrey Franz, interview.

[25]Willa Mae Gibson Mullins Moore, telephone interview by DruAnna Overbay, 3 January 2005.

When my dad was campaigning
to be reelected superintendent,
I would ride my trike around the yard
with my cousin Billie Mullins Horton,
urging all who passed
to "Vote for Drew B."

+ + + + +

Green

I remember the green organza dress
My mother bought me for my
Seventh Easter Sunday
And the too large white
Patent leather shoes I stuffed
With toilet paper in the toes
So they would fit.

I remember the feel of the dress,
Scratching my neck as I
Gathered Easter eggs from
The church lawn and
The envy I felt when
Dennis Trent found the prize egg—
The Easter basket with the
Plastic bunny and chocolate eggs
Should have been mine!!

(Remembering 1950 Life at Vardy after the Vardy School Reunion, 1998)

Chapter 15

Holidays

Members pictured on the church lawn after Easter services during the 1920s are, in the lower-right corner, Miss Rankin; left of the second row, Nancy Collins Miser and her sister Adelaide Collins Horton, Lizzie Horton Stewart, Hattie Bales, Grace Miser, Docia Collins Miser, and Little Alice Collins. Standing behind Grace and Docia is Alyce Horton. On the back row is Herbie Collins, an unidentified man, and Clay and Frank Miser. Immediately beyond on the right side corner of the church is Asa Gibson. Others are unidentified.

The children were encouraged to celebrate holidays and to participate in arts and crafts which depicted them. Among the ones most frequently mentioned were Halloween, Thanksgiving, Christmas, and Valentine's Day. Of course, other holidays were celebrated, such as New Year's and Abraham Lincoln's and George Washington's birthdays. During the early 1940s, the children wrote about these activities.

George Bell noted, "This week we in the upper grades are practicing the play we will give Thanksgiving."[1]

Even the first and second graders were excited to be in the play. "We are going to give a play for Thanksgiving and we are drawing turkeys," wrote Barbara Mullins.[2]

---

[1]George Bell, *Vardy School Newspaper* article.
[2]Barbara Mullins, *Vardy School Newspaper* article.

My older sister Charlotte wrote, "Since this is Christmas week, we have decorated our room. We have a pretty tree which is ready for Santa. On our tree we have snowballs. They are pretty and easy made. They are sycamore balls dipped in water and flour. D. H. Williams brought us a manger scene."[3]

Josephine Bell reported, "We have a pretty Christmas tree. Our tree has toys and birds in it. The boys made the birds in workshop. We have been making Santas to put up in our room. Ellis Mullins got a prize for doing the best work."[4]

Laura Mullins was one of the mothers who helped students in the community by making their costumes for school and church programs and special events.

Etta Jane Johnson's entry reads, "We are making Christmas pictures and coloring them. We have a lot of Santas under our tree. Miss Overton has been making the things for us to wear in our play."[5]

Dan Williams wrote, "This week we have been busy getting ready for Christmas. We drew names and we are going to exchange presents inside our room. D.H. Williams got the tree for our room. Johnnie Clyde Gibson brought Christmas decorations and helped decorate our room."[6]

VCHS members all spoke fondly of their Christmases at Vardy. Charles Sizemore recalled, "We always had a program of some kind at Christmas. We'd have plays and everyone got a box of hard candy. All of the younger children would get a small gift, and other than playing with my friends at recess, that was my fondest memory."[7]

---

[3]Charlotte Williams, *Vardy School Newspaper* article (Miss Tyler's room).
[4]Josephine Bell, *Vardy School Newspaper* article (Miss Miser's room).
[5]Etta Jane Johnson, *Vardy School Newspaper* article (Miss Overton's room).
[6]Daniel H. Williams, *Vardy School Newspaper* article.
[7]Charles Sizemore, Vardy Oral Histories.

"Every Christmas we had a Christmas party. Everybody got a gift. . . . We actually called it 'getting something off the Christmas tree' . . . and we looked forward to that. It wasn't much, but what little bit we got we really appreciated. I got a box of candy and a small toy," wrote Lloyd Williams.[8]

Hard Candy Christmas reunion in 1999 brought more alumni back to the center than any of the other reunions.

Audrey Mullins Franz told me, "Christmas—that was great. That was the time . . . we'd put on all these plays. We'd get all dressed up in our costumes, and we'd think we were in the movies. . . . We would work hard to get all of our parts done perfect so that when all of these people came to see us put on our plays, we'd be up there on stage showing off. It was great. We would have such a good time acting in the plays and doing all the other things that went along with the Christmas tree.

"But the most important thing was the little box of candy everybody got. All of the kids got a gift from the Christmas tree. Mr. and Mrs. Leonard and the church did it for us. We didn't go out and make up money to buy gifts for the children. They took care of it. The girls would some-times get a soft doll, and the boys would get a softball made out of socks. . . . [B]ut, it was beautiful. In years past I think maybe I got one doll that had hard arms and legs, but the rest of it was soft. That was probably bought. The rest of the stuff they probably worked and made. I don't know

[8]Lloyd Williams, Vardy Oral Histories.

how they did it. Maybe they had it sent in to them from Presbyterians. . . .
[T]hey really took care of us and that was wonderful."[9]

As a matter of fact, Mrs. Leonard's correspondence to various churches
throughout the Holston Presbytery as well as churches in Chicago, New
York, and Englewood Cliffs, New Jersey, brought many packages throughout the year that were carefully stored in the Rankin cottage. Just before
Halloween Mrs. Leonard, Miss Rankin, my mother Alyce Williams, Lillian
Grohse, Eliza Goins, and Stella Miser would begin going through the packages. There were tables set up in Miss Rankin's spare bedroom and in the
attic with each schoolchild's name written on an index card. The smaller
children got crayons and coloring books as well as toys and clothing.
Pencils and paper were always carefully wrapped in these packages along
with construction paper, scissors, and glue. Each child was treated fairly
and equally. When a choice had to be made of whether a child got a doll or
a new dress or pair of pants, the child who needed clothes got them.

Parents helped in the decision-making process when they would be
asked discreetly at church if the child needed a doll or a dress. Years later
the VCHS learned that some of the children did not understand this process
and had become a little upset if they "got an old dress" instead of a doll.
When all packages were opened and sorted, Mrs. Leonard wrote her friends
at Maryville College and asked for specific donations so that gifts could be
equitable.

As a result of the VCHS's hosting a school reunion remembering how
the church and community came together to celebrate Christmas, several
of those who attended Vardy School have shared stories of their experiences during those holidays. The following story is one of those.

My Hard Candy Christmas
(as told to Macie Mullins by her husband R. C. Mullins)

There was total darkness in our little home on top of Newman's
Ridge. The only noise to be heard was the old alarm clock ticking. My
excitement woke me early this day, for it was Christmas. I heard Mom
finally getting up. She lit the kerosene lamp, for we had no electricity,
and made her way to the fireplace to build a fire.

It was a cold winter morning. I lay there watching the fire burn in
the fireplace. I dared not come out from under the warm covers that

---

[9]Franz, Vardy Oral Histories.

took so long to get warm the night before. I was so excited I could hardly stand it. I just wanted to jump into my clothes and head for church, for it was at church that we would get our Christmas.

Artist Don Britton's pen-and-ink sketch of a Hard Candy Christmas at Vardy Church.

I heard Mom in the kitchen getting breakfast. The smell of ham frying and biscuits baking was more than I could stand. So, out of bed I rolled. It was so cold that I had to hurry to get dressed. I pulled on my bibbed overalls, and today I could wear my new shirt that Mom had made me. I tiptoed fast across the cold floor to the fireplace where Mom was warming our shoes and our socks.

I went into the kitchen to watch Mom as she fixed our breakfast. I pulled out one of the empty dynamite boxes that we used as seats and plopped myself down. Mom reminded me that it was Christmas day and I needed to get cleaned up so I would be ready for breakfast because we didn't want to be late for church.

I went to the washstand and poured a couple dipperfuls of cold water out of the water bucket into the wash pan. Mom brought over the tea kettle and poured enough hot water into the wash pan to make good warm water to wash. After I finished, I brushed my teeth and hair. I pulled back the curtains to look outside. It was breaking day. The rooster began to crow. Everything was covered with a blanket of snow for it had been snowing for two days.

It was finally time for breakfast. It seemed extra good this morning; Mom was a good cook. She got up and cleared the table and began getting ready for church. . . . It was finally time to go, so we all wrapped up real good for our journey down the ridge, across the footlog over Blackwater Creek, and through the field.

As I crossed the footlog, I saw Troy Williams heading toward the church. I yelled for him to wait up for me. Troy and I had been buddies for a long time. We had been in the same class together ever since the first grade.

Troy and I continued on to the church. As we opened the door and stepped into the foyer, we could smell Christmas. The big old cedar tree was being warmed by the Christmas lights and putting off a smell that was wonderful. We both were so excited as we stepped inside the church. Our eyes fastened onto the huge tree that went from the floor to the ceiling. It had lots of bright colored lights, decorations, little toys, and boxes of candy. It is a sight that has always stayed with me.

On this day Preacher Leonard would tell the Christmas story, and we would have plays and programs performed by the children. I could hardly wait till it was over so we could get our Christmas. The little box of hard candy was what I had waited for. I had not had any since last Christmas. My dad worked hard, but some days he worked all day for a dollar or less. There was not much work to be found in those days. So candy was a luxury we couldn't afford.

When I got my box of candy I hurried outside so I could open it. As I looked inside at all the pretty colored pieces, I took out one and placed it in my mouth. M-m-m, how good it was. I didn't dare bite into it, for I wanted it to last a long time.

That night as I lay in my bed with my two brothers I felt so grateful. I always had to share my bed with my two brothers and, most of the time, wear hand-me-down clothes. But, this little box of candy was all mine. I opened my eyes to take one more peep at my box of candy before going to sleep. Then I closed my eyes and felt such happiness inside. I hoped all little kids had their own box of candy, and that they had a wonderful Christmas like me.

Chapter 16

Wartime Contributions

From the Civil War to wars more recent, willing Vardy volunteers have served their country, but no conflict was remembered as much by those interviewed as World War II, for it was during 1943 that the Vardy Community Center honored twenty-eight servicemen and their families during a special service. Two services had to be held to accommodate all attendees. A service bulletin (printed program) kept these many years by former teacher and principal Mossie Kate Overton and given to the church museum lists the names of those men honored. They were Cass Alder, Wayland Alder, Carnell Bales, Boyd R. Collins, Bradley Collins, Clyde Collins, Homer Collins, Jay B. Collins, Mathis Collins, Oakey Collins, Pershing Collins, Ray H. Collins, Ray W. Collins, Rex Collins, David Collins, Elbert Davidson, James Davidson, Garfield Goins, Dailey Sexton, Simeon Goins, Ogle Moore, Chester Mullins, Jasper Mullins, Charlie Parks, Frank Parks, Patrick Parks, Roy Parks, and Wayland Saddler.[1]

Among the soldiers honored at Vardy's Service Flag Dedication were three sons of Herbie and Lizzie Collins: Boyd, Pershing ("Pet"), and Ray. Pet, shown here, and his brother Ray enlisted in the Army on August 24, 1936, and then reenlisted when World War II began. Ray was one of the soldiers who chauffeured General Patton.

Not only did these men join the war effort but many others did after these special services were held. One of those was Ruth Jenkins, who joined the WAVES (Women Accepted for Volunteer Emergency Service; they served in the Navy).

---

[1]Vardy Community Church bulletin, November 1943.

One can understand the full impact of those programs honoring Vardy servicemen by reading an article entitled "Vardy Dedicates Service Flag" in *The Church on the Hill*, the newsletter of the Presbyterian Church in Englewood, New Jersey. The following letter written by Reverend Leonard to Mr. Frederick S. Duncan, board of trustees, describes the services.

Our dedication of the Flag on Sunday was a real success. Over 500 were with us for the two services. In the morning worship service, I tried to emphasize the thought that while our men and women are fighting out battles across the sea, we are in danger of being so busy doing little no-account things that the greatest and finest moments of our lives may be lost. We had 'dinner on the grounds' and a short play time.

I was much impressed with the spirit of the afternoon service. All of the families of the boys were seated together. As I read the Roll of Honor, I had each group stand. Until that time I do not think our community knew just how close the war had come to us.

At the introduction of the dedication, I told of seeing your flag in Englewood; about my writing to learn where we could get one, and your reply. Then I read your letter. I am sure that did much to add to the worthwhileness of the day. You have not only given us this beautiful banner but have backed us up during these many years.[2]

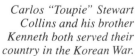

Boyd Collins was stationed in England during World War II and served in a hospital.

Carlos "Toupie" Stewart Collins and his brother Kenneth both served their country in the Korean War.

[2]Chester F. Leonard, letter to Fredrick S. Duncan, "Vardy Dedicates Service Flag," *The Church on the Hill* (November 1943).

When rationing became necessary, the minister announced a special meeting at the church for May 3, 1943. He explained the reasons for rationing and told the congregation, as nearly as possible, what information was needed by the registrars so that registration for ration books could be done accurately and quickly. The residents were registered at the Vardy School for "War Ration Book No. 1." From May 4 to May 7, 277 persons were registered.

Preacher Leonard recorded that "All were willing to cooperate and most work was done on the first two days. As each family was registered the name was put on the blackboard with the number of applications made and number of Ration Books issued."[3]

In addition to being responsible for the members to all get their fair share of ration coupons, the church/school leaders began a massive correspondence campaign. Every member of the community who could write as well as Vardy students joined with the church/school staff to write the servicemen. Many longtime friendships were forged among the younger students and the servicemen who became pen pals.[4]

The students wrote to more than thirty servicemen. When an answer was received, Preacher Leonard sent word to the family that the letter would be read in prayer meeting. Each Friday night three or four such letters were read. The location of the men, so far as known, was pointed out on the map, current news was given about the concerned places, and prayer was offered for the men in service and their families.

Prior to World War II, several Vardy residents had fought in World War I. Not only were Melungeons volunteers in these wars but also in those prior to it. My grandfather Daniel Boone Horton fought in the Spanish-American War. My step-grandmother Claribel is the sole surviving widow of a Spanish-American War veteran. To many Southern Melungeons, it is unbelievable that their ancestors fought for the Union during the Civil War. During a recent visit to our community, a Melungeon descendant argued with me that there was no way that our mutual great-grandfather Batey Collins had been in the Northern army. I was surprised since she had just been to the Vardy Community Cemetery and had taken a photograph of his tombstone. Evidently she hadn't read it, for his tombstone states that he had

---

[3]Chester F. Leonard, Vardy Community Presbyterian church records, May 1943.

[4]"As Others See Him," *The Church on the Hill* (January 1944).

been in the "Union Army Company E of the Tennessee Calvary," as had many other Vardy residents.

Many of the records that Bill Grohse kept listed several Vardy residents who had been involved in the conflict. There are many research sources from which to obtain information about these voluntary servicemen, including Jean Patterson Bible's *Melungeons Yesterday and Today*.

Several of those who participated in this project have laughingly remarked that even those who are their neighbors in their Northern homes have found it unbelievable that their forebears were Union sympathizers.

Despite the large numbers of Vardy residents who were Union soldiers and sympathizers, there were those who joined the Southern cause. True to the image of the Civil War, neighbors and even relatives fought against each other.

Sue Sizemore recently told me, "According to our family records, Charles's maternal grandfather, Jeremiah (Jerry) M. Mullins, was in Company B 50th Virginia Infantry for the Confederate States Army. He enlisted in April 1861, for twelve months in Jonesville, Lee County, Virginia, and then reenlisted May 1, 1862."[5]

Both Ruth Jenkins and her brother Frank were in World War II. Ruth was in the Navy WAVES and Frank was in the Army, fighting in the Pacific theater.

---

[5]Sue Sizemore, personal comments about Jeremiah M. Mullins's Civil War Service Documentation, to DruAnna Overbay, Spring 2003.

+ + + + +

Alzheimer's Agony

"Peggy was born in Japan,"
And the conversation began.
"Where have you been?" I asked.
"I was worried about you."
She turned to her husband,
"We came straight here," he laughed.

"Peggy was born in Japan,"
And the argument began,
"No, she was born in Germany,"
Her husband corrected her.
"Oh yes, she responded,
"We lived in Japan when our troops
Occupied Japan after THE WAR.
I remember now . . . I went to Tito's trial—
You should have been there," she said
And began recounting the trial that
She had told me about hundreds
Of times before. Vivid details
Made me sit in her chair at the trial.
There was a pause.

"Peggy was born in Japan."
And his accusation began.
"She's getting worse," her husband confided,
"I don't know if you've noticed or not."
How could I not?
My closest friend of twenty-five years,
My confidant, my mentor—how could
This happen to such a lovely person?

"Peggy was born in Japan,"
And his anger began.
"My God," he said. "Will
You get off that kick? You
Have told her that fifty times today,
And you know she was born in Germany!"

He screamed,
She recoiled into herself.

"Peggy wasn't born in Japan,"
She looked at me, tears glistening.
"And, he kept getting lost coming
To your house . . . we started over
At least a hundred times . . . I finally
Got him back to Wal-Mart and then
I made him listen to me as I told
Him which way to turn. That's why
We are late—he forgot the way . . .
I put my arms around her and kissed
Her cheek.
"Peggy is your age."
She did remember that.

(After my friend's last visit before moving
to a nursing home in Birmingham, 1994)

Chapter 17

Historical Register Placement

An inventory for the nomination of the Vardy Community Presbyterian Center's placement on the National Register of Historic Places done in November 1978 lists fifteen buildings in the Vardy School Community District. The list included the church, the school, the second mission school, the manse, two bungalows, a general store, a summer cottage, a library, a bath house, a storage house, two garages, a shed, and a water-storage-tank house. However, this inventory had included several neighboring buildings that were not built with Presbyterian Mission or community funds. Among these were, listed as numbers six and thirteen, the house and garage of my parents, Alyce and Drew Williams, which were built in 1934, and the general store, erected in 1937.

After the restoration of the church, the relocation and restoration of the Mahala Log Cabin began in the spring of 2000. On hand for the groundbreaking were David Collins, Anthony Collins, W. C. Collins, Charles Sizemore, Macie Mullins, R. C. Mullins, O. H. Collins, DruAnna Overbay, Fred Overbay, and Theresa Burchett.

Today there are only seven buildings remaining, all of which, with the exception of the church house, are privately owned and/or occupied by Batey Collins' descendants: the deteriorating schoolhouse and summer house are owned by my sister, brothers, and me; the second mission school built in 1902, occupied by Sharon Johnson (Frankie's great granddaughter);

bungalow (mission house, circa 1920), occupied by David Collins and his sister Ruby (grandchildren of Frankie); and the Chester F. Leonard Manse and clinic (library), owned by my husband and me (granddaughter of Adelaide). The other buildings have been ravaged by deterioration, and some are completely gone.

Other DNA study participants Dan H. Williams, R. C. Mullins, and Troy Williams were anxious to have conclusive evidence of their ancestors.

After the mission work at Vardy ceased, several situations arose that the community had been unaware of, resulting from the fact that Batey Collins deeded the property to the Presbyterians only on condition that when and if the school and church were no longer being held, then his descendants would equally inherit the right to redeem the property.

Attached to church records and written in Mary J. Rankin's handwriting is the limiting or restraining clause of the deed. When the Leonards left, they had carefully researched what could happen to the property in the event that the Presbyterians left. Citing from the Tennessee Law Digest (Code of Tennessee, 1932), found in Martindale-Hubbell Law Dictionary (1951) volume 2, Law Digest, the Leonards and their lawyer sent the following information to Batey's grandchildren.

> Real property not acquired by descent from a parent or other ancestor by gift, devise, or descent, descends: (1) To children and/or issue of deceased children by representation;xxx (Sec. 8380).

> (Above means that real property of a deceased person would descend, first to his children, and if he were survived, for instance, by one child and by three children of a deceased child, the child would take one/half and the three grandchildren would each take one/third of the remaining one/half.)

The letter continues on a more personal note from the Leonards:

> This clearly shows that Nancy, Adelaide, Frankie, and Noah would equally 'inherit' the right to be equal heirs to redeem property under a limiting or restraining clause. Nancy has one share; Adelaide has one share; Frankie has one share; and Noah has one share.
>
> This complication of many grandchildren banded together looks as if no one could untangle the knot. Just who would have the right to buy? You are all heirs to the right to buy—Grandpaw Beaty (Batey) could not look into the 'factions' he was creating. Frankly, the Board has a nice question of law on its hands if it ever attempts to sell.

At the 1998 Vardy reunion held at the church, board members recognized were (front row) Macie Mullins; W. C. Collins, VCHS treasurer; DruAnna Overbay, secretary; Troy Williams, president; and Molly Hall. On the back row were R. C. Mullins, Willie Grohse, Ronald Lambert, Charles Sizemore, Anthony Collins, and Fred Overbay.

Even though the Presbyterian Board of National Missions had given the school property to the Hancock County Board of Education, they had no legal right to do so. When school no longer was held on the property, an auction among the interested descendants was held.

In the fall of 2000, VCHS members gathered to appreciate the relocation and restoration of the Mahala Mullins Log Cabin, some of whom are her descendants. Seated on the porch are Theresa Burchett, C. M. and Sally Collins, O. H. Collins and his friend Annie, Anne Callahan, and W. C. Collins. On the back are DruAnna Overbay, Jim Callahan, and R. C. Mullins.

Only two descendant families were interested: the sole surviving daughter Nancy Miser and her niece (my mother) Alyce Williams. Mom and Dad purchased the Rankin Cottage, and when the school was auctioned, their bid purchased the school. When the church was no longer in use, Mattie Mae and Willie Grohse (Nancy Miser's grandson) purchased the church and the manse.

As late as 1996, the option for only Batey Collins's descendants to hold personal deeds to the properties has been honored when Willie Grohse sold the church and manse to DruAnna Overbay. Both are great-grandchildren of Batey Collins.

Vardy Community Historical Society

The fall of 1996 brought many of the Vardy students together at Elm Springs Baptist Church's recreation hall for their first school reunion. Persistent determination by Vardy School alumnus Eliza Johnson Collins to have a reunion finally became a reality after she asked W. C. Collins to organize the effort. Having lost touch with so many of their friends down through the years made this a poignant moment in the students' lives and one that they wished to expand. Reminiscing about their days at Vardy inspired W. C. Collins to suggest that the group purchase a bronze marker to show their appreciation to the Vardy Community School's staff and spiritual leaders. Troy Williams passed the hat to collect money to purchase the marker. Suggesting that a five-member committee work on the wording and placement of the marker, various alumni called out names of those they felt should serve on it. Added to the names of W. C. Collins and Troy Williams were the names of DruAnna Overbay, Alvin Mullins, and John Mullins. Few realized that at that moment the Vardy Community Historical Society had been launched.

Charles Sizemore, the second VCHS board president, installed in 2000, receives a revised set of the organization's bylaws from Troy Williams, the 1998 charter president.

When the committee met after the reunion, the question of where the marker would be placed was brought up. For a number of months, my husband and I had discussed purchasing the church house and manse from Willie and Mattie Mae Grohse and had placed on it an option to buy. Realizing that the most appropriate placement of the marker would be on the Vardy Church property, I mentioned that I would sell the church to the group if I indeed purchased the property, provided that the group formed the Vardy Community Historical Society (VCHS). W. C. Collins was asked if he thought there could possibly be grant funds to do so.

In January 1997, the Overbays purchased the property. W. C. Collins and Jack Mullins had sought grant monies from the Nature Conservancy to help with the funding. The selling price of the church was $10,000. The committee met again in the fall of 1997, with two more members—Jack Mullins and O. H. Collins—being added to the roundtable discussion. In order to obtain the grant money, the historical society had to be officially established and registered with the State of Tennessee as well as the IRS. O. H. Collins hired his lawyer in Mountain City to look over the charter and bylaws that the group had formulated. After approval of the charter and by-laws, the papers were filed with the state. In January 1998, the State of Tennessee granted the VCHS charter. Meanwhile W. C. Collins, Troy Williams, and DruAnna Overbay filed the IRS application to be named a nonprofit organization. The receipt of that status in April of that year was cause for celebration.

Troy Williams and R. C. Mullins are dressed in nifty-50s style for the 2000 Vardy alumni reunion. Note the restored curved window which was characteristic of the architecture of the Mahala Mullins Log Cabin.

The Nature Conservancy granted $5,000, which the group was able to immediately match. After the Overbays received the purchase price of the church, they donated $5,000 back to the organization so that repairs could begin. Additional board members were sought to help with the endeavor. Willie Grohse, R. C. Mullins, Charles Sizemore, and Anthony Collins were among the first group of board members to continue working together for the restoration. Since the organization of the board in 1998, four members are now deceased: Alvin Mullins, John Mullins, Willie Grohse, and Bill Miser.

Since its founding in 1998, the VCHS has completed several major projects. The first was the restoration of the Vardy Church so that school and family reunions could take place there. Troy Williams, president of the VCHS, spearheaded that effort. During the restoration period, Dr. C. M. Lipsey, a former visiting minister at Vardy, obtained a $10,000 grant from Humanities Tennessee (Tennessee Humanities Council) to transfer old glass lantern slides into large photographs, which are now hanging in the church. Along with that grant, the board was to collect oral histories of the Vardy residents and former students. Approximately thirty-seven taped histories have been completed. Those taped memories and photographs are the basis of this book.

Aunt Mahala Mullins's descendants, Ruth Muhlbauer and her niece, discuss the recording of their oral histories with me and another descendant, author of Lest We Forget, *Jim Callahan.*

After the church was restored, Dan Williams donated the Mahala Log Cabin to the organization, provided that it be moved from Newman's Ridge so that it would be more accessible to the public. Charles Sizemore was the president of the organization. Jack Mullins and W. C. Collins were appointed by the board to oversee the "Aunt Mahala Log Cabin Project." A grant of $5,600 from Clinch-Powell Resource Conservation and Development (RC&D) Council was received on a matching funds contingency to help finance the project. Those returning to the reunion that fall were amazed to see that the cabin had not only been moved to a site across from the church but that it had been almost completely restored.

To fund the "Windows on the Past" traveling exhibit of the large photographs that hang in the Vardy Church Museum, VCHS received a $1,000 matching funds grant from the East Tennessee Foundation in 2003. The exhibit portrays life in the Melungeon community of Vardy and has traveled throughout the four states of Tennessee, Virginia, Kentucky, and North Carolina, stopping at seven colleges as well as churches and museums.

Colleges which served as hosts of the exhibit are King College, Bristol, Tennessee; Union College, Barbourville, Kentucky; Virginia Intermont, Bristol, Virginia; Warren Wilson College, Swannanoa, North Carolina; Pikeville College, Pikeville, Kentucky; and Carson-Newman College, Jefferson City, Tennessee. The East Tennessee History Museum in Knoxville, Tennessee, and the Rose Center in Morristown, Tennessee were also hosts of the exhibit.

Phyllis Trent Meyer, David Trent, Beuna Trent O'Connor, Euna Trent Francisco, and Dennis Trent enjoy exchanging memories of growing up in Vardy, experiences they shared with other Vardy alumni during the 1999 reunion.

Eight Vardy reunions, including the one in 2004, will have taken place by the time this book is published: the first in 1996, at Elm Springs; the second in the dilapidated church in 1998; the third in 1999, called "A Hard Candy Christmas"; the fourth in 2000, called "Let the Good Times Roll"; the fifth in 2001, known as "Old Fashion Days"; the sixth in 2002, named "Good Times, Good Memories"; the seventh, in 2003 became "School Days"; and the eighth, in 2004, was "A Gospel Sing by Vardy Alumni." Additionally, in February 1999, a centennial celebration of the church building's marking its one-hundredth year brought a full house of former students and residents back to Vardy. One has only to look at the church and Mahala Log Cabin to know that the organization is a viable one. The East Tennessee Historical Society and other organizations have given awards for VCHS efforts.

Katie Doman noted that "An astonishing number of former Vardy students make the trip to the valley each year for the reunions, honoring their former educators, the family members who supported them in their education efforts, and each other. These people keep remarkable track of one another, and many of them have extraordinary stories to tell—stories that offer insight into how they maintain such a strong sense of community, even when the members of the VCHS live in places scattered all over the United States.

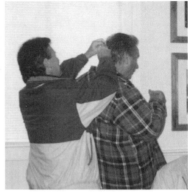

Vardy Community Historical Society readily participated in the DNA studies which Dr. Brent Kennedy had initiated. Kennedy is shown here pulling a hair sample, roots and all, from Jack Mullins.

"Now they hope that by restoring the church as a museum and rebuilding the Mahala Log Cabin in the valley, they can entice people from the outside world to come to the valley and hear their stories, taking away a sense of the community's history and culture. The VCHS members hope to continue the educational legacy left to them by the Presbyterians as they work together to document and preserve their community traditions—and to pass them on to visitors."[1]

The mission of the Vardy Community Historical Society, Inc. is to record and report on the lives, times, and culture of the people living in the Vardy Valley along Blackwater Creek in East Tennessee; to document the Presbyterians' contributions to the health, education, and religious needs of the resident families from 1862 to 1974; to restore and maintain certain properties of historical interest built during the late nineteenth and early twentieth; and to participate with individuals, groups, and educational institutions with like interest in the origins, migration, and lives of people living in Vardy and elsewhere known as Melungeons.[2]

Because of our mission, as well as our own curiosity about our roots, we have participated in the DNA studies correlated by Dr. Brent Kennedy, who was in the fall of 2000 the vice-chancellor at the University of Virginia's College at Wise. VCHS eagerly agreed to Kennedy's proposal that we become subjects of the DNA studies.

---

[1]Katie Doman, submitted manuscript to *Windows on the Past*, 20 June 2002.

[2]VCHS Mission Statement, at <http://hometown.aol.com/vardyvalley/vchs mission.html>.

Hosting the Melungeon Heritage Association's annual meeting on June 23, 2001, has been one of the VCHS highlights. When Connie Clark, the president of the organization at that time, approached the board concerning the MHA proposal to meet at Vardy, the board was very receptive. The commonality of the two groups has enhanced both organizations.

Vardy School alumni all remember the Hard Candy Christmases they enjoyed at Vardy.

+ + + + +

Melungeon Ancestry Mystery

Your great ole aunt Sukie was right, Mama
I wish you could know
That when she rambled on saying,
"Me? Why I'm Port-uh-gee"
She was right, Mama.

I wish you could know
That in unraveling the mystery
Scholars now talk about
The forgotten settlers who came
In 1567 with Juan Pardo
Settling in what is now East Tennessee—
The names of those,
From the archives in Portugal,
Included one called, "Collingso."

I wish you could know
That despite the sneers of
"She's one of them Melungeons
From Hancock County" remarks
I look them in the eye with a
"You damned well better not forget it" stare.

I wish you could know and be pleased
That I wear my ancestry with pride
Smeared with Campbell County coal dust.
I wish you, too,
Could have held your head high
And claimed our ancestry.

(After hearing Brent Kennedy speak at McClung Museum in 1992)

Appendix A

Genealogy

The following genealogy charts should help the reader understand the Melungeon lines to which I trace my ancestry.

Collins Lines

Vardemon Collins (1764–?)	m. (ca. 1798)	Margaret "Peggy" Gibson (1773–?)
Alfred Collins (1810–?)	m. (?)	Elizabeth Mullins (1812–?)
Batey (Baty) Collins (1843–1914)	m. (?)	Cynthia Collins or Goins (1845–1930)
Adelaide Collins (1872–1931)	m. (1904)	Daniel Boone Horton (1882–1966)
Alyce Horton (1909–1991)	m. (1930)	Drew Butler Williams (1907–1998)

DruAnna Elizabeth Williams Overbay (1942–)

Some stories about Grandmother Cynthia's parentage state that Grandmother Frankie was pregnant with Cynthia when Simeon died. If my Grandmother Cynthia's father was Simeon Collins then the line would be as follows.

Vardemon Collins (1764–?)	m. (ca. 1798)	Margaret "Peggy" Gibson (1773–?)
Simeon Collins (1803–1843)	m. (?)	Frankie Bunch (1805–1885)
Cynthia Collins (1843–1930)	m. (?)	Batey (Baty) Collins (1845–1914)
Adelaide Collins (1872–1931)	M. (1904)	Daniel Boone Horton (1882–1966)
Alyce Horton (1909–1991)	m. (1930)	Drew Butler Williams (1907–1998)

DruAnna Elizabeth Williams Overbay (1942–)

Goins Line

In other family stories, Grandmother Frankie did not have her daughter Cynthia until two years after Simeon's death. Frankie's common-law husband was John Hammer Goins who became the husband of Lucinda Sexton sometime during the late 1850s. If my grandmother Cynthia's father was John Hammer Goins as some genealogists suggest, then the line would be as follows.

Alexander Goins (1815—1870)	m. (?)	Ethie Collins (1810–1880)
John Hammer Goins (1833–1900)	and	Frankie Bunch (1805–1885)
Cynthia Collins (1845–1930)	m. (?)	Batey (Baty) Collins (1845–1914)
Adelaide Collins (1845–1930)	m. (1904)	Daniel Boone Horton (1882–1966)
Alyce Horton (1909–1991)	m. (1930)	Drew Butler Williams (1907–1998)

DruAnna Elizabeth Williams Overbay (1942–)

Ethie Collins in this line is the daughter of Vardemon Collins and Margaret "Peggy" Gibson.

Bunch Line

Frankie Bunch's parents were Benjamin Bunch and Mary Dotson.

Leonard's Love Letters

The external life of an individual often paints a very different picture than that of his internal life. It is hard to understand another unless we look at both aspects. In writing and interpreting various documents concerning the life of Chester F. Leonard, by listening to others tell about his impact on their lives as well as remembering the minister that I knew as a child, there has been nothing which has really made me feel as if I really knew him that can compare to words he has written. Church records of his reports and sermons have been especially helpful in seeing inside the mind of our beloved minister. Correspondence to my parents, his friends, and to others opened a window into the man's heart. However, the purity of that heart is only exemplified by reading letters he wrote to his beloved. True, he never intended any eyes but Josephine's to read these words, and while others may consider the publishing of these letters as being too invasive into his personal life, I believe they really show a man who followed the words of his Lord.

Leonard Love Letter 1

Tuesday, sometime before Night class

Dearest Little Kiddie:—

Your last two letters came right thru just as they should and, Lady, they didn't stop at the eye but went right on to my heart. How more can I tell you my appreciation of your picture. Will you think me foolish when I tell you that an almost uncontrollable desire makes me almost worship the face of it. It is no wonder to me at all that some people make fatal mistakes because of longing for something or someone.

Perhaps, lady, it is the cares and the little worries that have taken up their abode in room 59 that make me need a cheerful companion for a change and you have sent yourself. May the Lord give you the comfort that your love gives me and a thousand fold more.

And the flowers. I took them home for mother, and dad, and Florence to see. My! but I was proud of them. But, Jop, you should see me as I told of your grades. Nell could hardly be more proud of her babe than I of my pal and tho they say mother's love is strongest—mine is running a close second. You put a test to it once by asking a question and I stood the test though afterwards it caused me to think. Later, I decided that my answer was correct. No matter what happens be sure of the fellow who has been allowed to treat you already as his wife, that's me. Often do I wonder at what we did but it was a lesson to me and one which shall be often used in our ministry.

Josephine, have you noticed a certain weakening lately, a greater desire for being loved, less of that old snap which I used to have? Perhaps I just imagine that I'm losing ground and grip. Goodness! it would be great to know that it was only my own idea for if I stand present strains with even backing up a little all of my ministry can't back me down.

Had a strange experience the other night, Saturday. All day my head wanted to burst but I wouldn't let it for there was much work for the next day which was Easter. That night I had a spell like at Xmas. Just wide awake dreaming and aching. Then I prayed that you might come and calm me and hold me as I slept. And, kiddie, you came even as I prayed; even before sleep found me and stayed. Several times seemingly wakening I found you present and bidding me sleep. Have you ever felt that way?

Seldom [ ] I drea[ ] this [ ] happening when it would do so much good in providing necessary rest seems to be one of those answer to prayers.

Do you believe it could have been?

Class

Must just write a little more and then crawl in for to-morrow. I must begin my service for my strength is returning and the morrow should see me again ready for a man's job.

Lady, my health has not been specially [ ] [ ] the North and the Lord has been specially kind in helping me as He has. You know that. If I stand another month the mountain will soon put me back on my feet where I belong.

While I think of it, would it be worth the money for me to come to M.C. on my way to the mission field. You know I shall be in Hancock County all summer. It all depends on how much time we can have together. If I do get there it would be from Friday (April 7) to Wednesday. I think [ ] [ ] until after [ ] I think.

Of course, the board may want me at once. Then there will be no chance of my seeing you so don't plan on it except to tell me if you think it worthwhile and don't work up any enthusiasm over the idea.

Now, I must quit for to-night and crawl out at 4 o'clock (3 correct time).

I don't mind the change do you.

Love you? Well I guess yes.

Chet

+ + + + +

Leonard Love Letter 2

Dear Josephine Wicks:—

The cancellation on this envelope will tell you how far this came and where I had arrived when this was mailed, probably, Tazewell. I am so delighted with your progress and so glad that you will soon be on your last lap toward home. Things will seem very different when I know that you are at the house and I have something to go down there for. That is poor English but right. Perhaps, then, I can settle down to work again and get something done.

I shall merely try to keep things going this next week and then after that I'll not have so much running around to do until after school is over.

My dear, everyone has been very kind to us and yet it is not the same as our having the opportunity of trying to be kind to each other. I shall be very awkward and often in a hurry but I shall do my best—and in the past have tried to do what was possible. There are so many things that make that best possible not seem to amount to much but that makes little difference—always that which merely "seems" has been so inadequate for me. If we could get to what is real and what counts then maybe I would be satisfied. Always I have had to do what others said should be done—someday I may do what I know needs to be done. But I love you so that it hurts. My dear, you will soon be with me again.

Your lover
CFL

+ + + + +

Leonard Love Letter 3

Sunday Night—9:00

Dear Josephine Wicks:—

I love you more than you can ever know. I have been with you few hours to-day when we were both tired. This note will be mailed so that you will have a little of my company after I am gone.

My dear, twenty years ago I loved you so much that I could hardly stand having you out of my sight—yet, for many months you lived in the South while I was in Chicago. For a month this past season I have dreaded that separation that had to be—but if it gives you back to me well and stronger than before—I am happy.

I thank the Lord each day for giving you to me these several years and I ask him to teach me to be kind and unselfish.

My impatience is not meanness but an inner driving force that must work itself out lest something breaks.

I shall be back at work but I shall think of you often.

My beloved, don't worry about getting home. I'll take you as soon as I think it is safe. I shall spend as much time as I can with you here. I am so glad that each day finds you more like yourself.

Remember now and always that I have loved you and do love you.

Your lover

Some Leonard Archives

A sermon: "Why Join the Church" (Vardy, 26 August 1934)

WHY JOIN THE CHURCH: Matt. 10:32-33.   Vardy, August 26, 1934.

I DON'T SEE WHY I SHOULD JOIN A CHURCH: I CAN LIVE AS GOOD A LIFE WITHOUT THAT
    I wish to give you, if you are a Christian, the reasons why people should
    join the church. Of course, if you are not a Xian, you have no reason.

Requires I. JESUS REQUIRES THAT WE CONFESS HIM BEFORE PEOPLE:
       What would you think of one who claimed to be your friend when alone
       but was ashamed of you when others were about? Not very friendly.
    Jesus said: COME FOLLOW ME: taught them His love, helpfulness, life.
      THEY COULD NOT FOLLOW JESUS LONG WITHOUT LETTING FOLKS KNOW IT:
      Then He said: EVERYONE: THEREFORE: WHO SHALL CONFESS ME BEFORE MEN,
          HIM ALSO SHALL I CONFESS BEFORE MY FATHER WHO IS IN H---
          BUT WHOSOEVER SHALL DENY ME BEFORE MEN: HIM ALSO WILL
          I DENY BEFORE MY FATHER WHO IS IN HEAVEN.
    Then the first test of belief, faith, IS CONFESSION BEFORE PEOPLE:
    WILLINGNESS TO BE DIFFERENT FOR JESUS: If not willing, not worthy of Him.

Strengthens II. BELONGING WITH OTHERS STRENGTHENS AND BLESSES US:
& livelihood   Doing anything hard alone is almost impossible: two can do better than 1.
    LIVING THE CHRISTIAN LIFE IS NOT EASY: one cannot drift along; one cannot
    be without care; IF WE JOIN WITH OTHERS TRYING TO LIVE RIGHTLY IT MAKES
    IT EASIER FOR ALL OF US:
    TELLING OTHERS OF HOW WE HAVE BEEN HELPED ADDS TO OUR BLESSINGS:
Blessing WOMAN TOUCHED JESUS' CLOTHING: healed: Who touched me: none knew except woman.
& added   Afraid she came up and said: I DID: SIR. GO IN PEACE: YOU ARE MADE WHOLE.
      Added to healing of body was mind at rest, and spirit at peace with God.
      PERSONAL WORD FROM THE SON OF GOD.

Helps III. JOINING THE CHURCH HELPS OTHERS.
Others HAVE YOU NOTICED HOW A SERVICE LIKE THIS SETS ALL THINKING:????
    THOSE ALREADY MEMBERS: look back to time they confessed: Am I doing as
    I should; have I lived up to my promises: WISH I COULD BE BETTER: I SHALL.
    THOSE WHO HAVE NEVER ACCEPTED JESUS: I wonder if there is something in it;
    I want to be better, finer, all that I can be. I WONDER IF THIS IS THE WAY
    ONE WHO IS ABOUT TO JOIN TELLS IT: another says: IF YOU DO I SHALL: ready
    but waiting to make up mind; and so we have all of these.
    ALL IN THE COMMUNITY HAVE HAD SOMETHING WORTH WHILE TO THINK ABOUT.

Do more IV. BY JOINING THE CHURCH WE CAN DO MORE FOR JESUS:
    WE WANT TO SHOW OUR CARE AND LOVE FOR HIM BY HELPING HIM IN HIS WORK:
    WE ARE HIS FRIENDS AND WANT TO PROVE IT: 2 are stronger than 1; 10-2;
    50-10; 70-50. All working for the peace, welfare of Community.
    THIS CHURCH STANDS FOR CHRISTIAN LIVING:
      helping people around us to be happy, healthy, strong in body, mind, spirit
      giving boys, girls, men, women, an opportunity to be the best they can be.
    EVERY FAITHFUL MEMBERS ADDS TO THE STRENGTH OF THE RIGHT KIND OF CHURCH:

Not for is V. THERE ARE PLENTY OF PEOPLE STANDING AROUND OUTSIDE:
against   ready to find fault; to criticize; to tear down; to ruin.
    They did the same for Jesus in His day.
         IF YOU ARE A CHRISTIAN YOU CAN HELP HIM MUCH BY JOINING HIS
         CHURCH AND TRYING TO HELP IN THE BUILDING UP OF HIS KINGDOM:
    JESUS SAID: HE THAT IS NOT FOR ME IS AGAINST ME:
      there is no standing at the door of His Kingdom and looking in;
      no sitting outside and expecting Him to count you among those present;
      As far as His work is concerned you are either inside or out;
      either for or against.

Love letter a

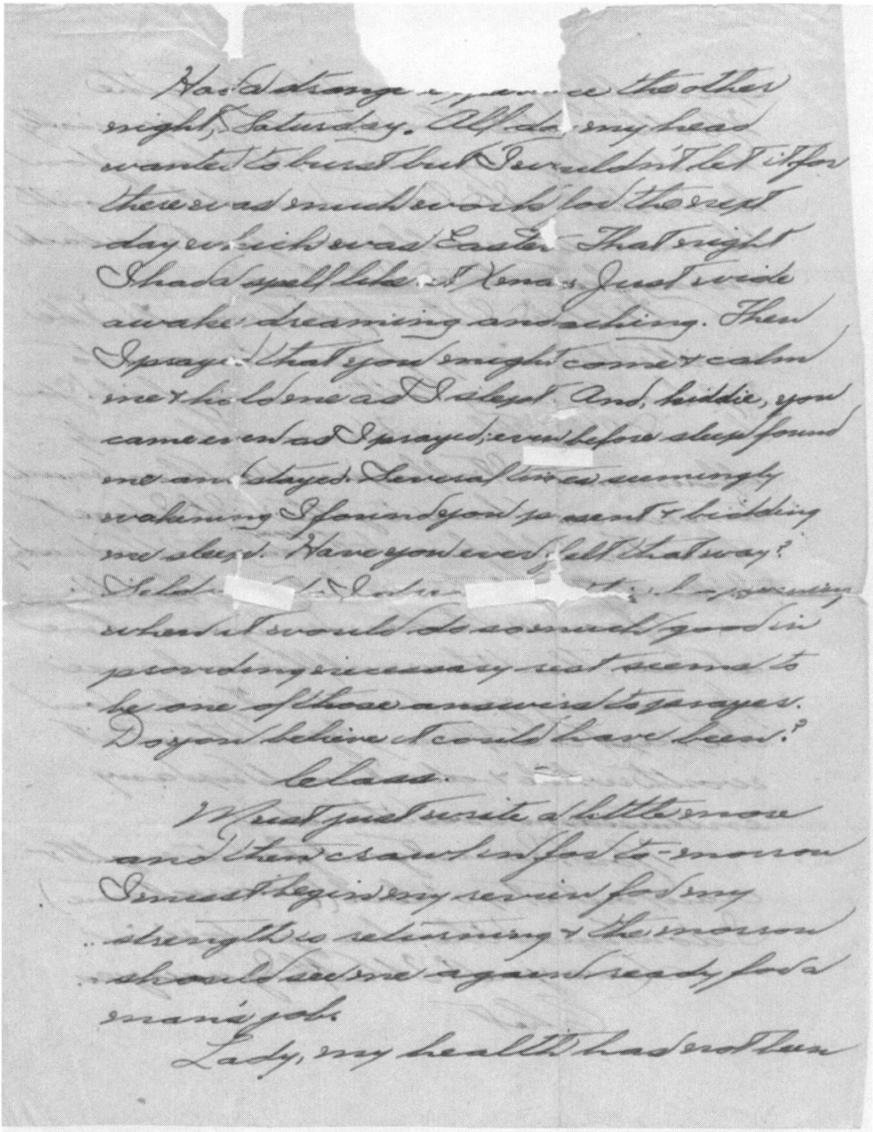

Love letter b

Pencil page front

Pencil page back

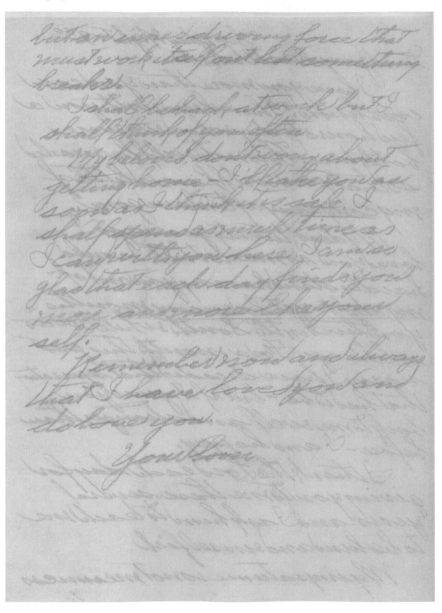

Appendix C

Stuart Correspondence

Publishing the letters Jesse Stuart wrote in response to mine, I believe, will shed new light on his writing of *Daughter of the Legend*. My father remembered during one of Stuart's visits to my parents' home that Stuart sat on the front porch looking up to Aunt Mahala's log cabin on Newman's Ridge while writing furiously in his little notebook. (This visit was sometime during the 1930s, after my parents' new house was built and long before I was born.)

Dad explained that Stuart had carried a little notebook in his shirt pocket and whenever he saw something or heard something unusual, he would pull the notebook from his pocket and begin writing. Stuart, Dad told me, did this even when they were roommates at Lincoln Memorial University. Constantly taking notes about how something or someone looked, Stuart then referred to his notes to facilitate his descriptive writing. Encouraged by that lesson, I began taking notes about our family and friends.

JESSE HILTON STUART
RIVERTON, KY.
BACHELOR OF ARTS

Gamma Lambda Sigma '26-'27-'28-'29, Vice-President '26, Secretary '27, Treasurer '28, Art Critic '29; Glee Club '27; Track '28-'29; Kentucky Club '27-'28-'29, Vice-President '28; Student Volunteer Band '27-'28, Treasurer '27, Secretary '28; Y.M.C.A. '27-'28; Dramatic Club '29; Writer's Club '29; Blue and Gray '26-'27-'28-'29, Editor-in-Chief '28-'29.

He does not need the spectacles of books to read nature. He does not need the precedent of others intellect to be intellectual. He conquers adversity with the same zeal that he enjoys prosperity. In this aspiring, determined man genius does not lie dormant. In the future Stuart must inevitably occupy the Pinnacle with America's greatest poets.

"What price Glory?"

Because Dad had put on his Lincoln Memorial University application that he enjoyed writing poetry, Jesse Stuart chose him for his roommate in 1927. LMU asked juniors and seniors to room with newly arriving freshmen to mentor them through their first two years. The son of a coal miner living in Harlan, Kentucky, at the time, made Dad a perfect fit. They enjoyed each other's company during those two years.

Jesse Stuart
Greenup,Ky.

Druanna Overbay,
916 Grace Ave.,
Lake City,Tenn.

Greenup,Kentucky
Nov.13th 1966

Drunna Overbay,
916 Grace Avenue,
Lake City,Tenn.

Dear Miss Overbay:

Your letter is excellent and I am happy you have
written me. But I disagree with you that I should have left out of
Daughter of the Legend, the number of suppositions, carried everwhere
about the origin of the Melungeons. If I had done this,I would have
defeated the purpose of The Daughter of the Legend.It's wonderful to
be born of a race that doesn't know its origin.I have traveled over
most of the world, and while I do not know all about the races of
various countries where I have been,I don't know of any race that
cannot find it's origin,.just the Melungeons,.and this is what that
makes then unique. I'll say in another fifty to onehundred years there
will be no Melungeons.They are going rapidly by intermarriage.
I think it would be rather interesting, if not
wonderful to have been born a Melungeon.
Look at the treatment they received.It was
terrible.People know it now.My dear young Miss Overbay I knew them
long before you were born. I went there first in 1926,a young man,
almost a boy, 19, I believe.I loved them.No road on Newman's Ridge. I
climbed the mountain..paths going up there. Today they're about all
Baptists,nice brick churches, hard surfaced roads, automobiles.
my wife who has shopped on Fifth Ave.NYC, Lord and Taylors, shopped
in the new Sneedville.Found a few things too. No one knew us. I
wanted to go back and see the country of my youth.I wrote the book
in 1941.It wasn't published until 1965.Your father, Drew Williams and
I worked many a day together on the LMU campus.
I think it was terrible to have barred Melungeons
from the solid white schools.In a town in Kentucky close the Tenn.border
one family of Melungeons lived.They were barred from both white and
colored schools. The Melungeons never have to worry about me. I cursed
under my breath at their treatment.It made me mad as hell then and I said,
so help me God, if I lived I'd do an immortal book for them.The question
is, have I done it? You should see the real good letters I get from over
America on this book,yet it got some nasty reviews from I'm not saying
where...but not from East Tennessee..all from that area were splendid.
But it's a region I know and love and have so many friend s because my
youth is there and it's an area of America where I could have lived all
my days..yes,Hancok or Hawkins counties or any of the rest in that area.
In two reviews of this book it was mentioned the
Melungeons were part Negro. I immediately sent letters to the reviewers.
There is a dictionary that gives this definition (you check and see)
and I wondered where this was coming from.I think it should be changed.
No one knows who they are.But I will say,I believe, there is plenty of
Cherokee Indian blood in them, juding from the straight black hair and
high sheek bones. The minute my wife saw one she said:"Jesse, they're
Indian and caucasian."The reason they didn't progress,reason they were
said to be clannish,and so are we Kentucky mountaineers,is the reason
we were and are hemmed in. Melungeons didn't have a chance,not as much
as we Kentucky mountaineers.They were branded by race.
I had in this book a few other things which were
removed before publication.I had in it about the trial they won about
diesegration.I had and perhaps still have a record of it.They won,I am

2
sure, over the State of Tennessee and went to white schools before the
Supreme Court's Decision to made mandatory diesegreation in all public
schools.Melungeons asked the State to tell them who they were.To prove
it.State couldn't.So they won,I had in the book the Melungeons were not
any part Negro. Did you know this would have shown bias,regarding
the Negro,.according to laws in America...and I had to take this out.
So I say it doesn't matter about the opinion so much as it does what
the Melungeon is now and what he does.I'd like for the Melungon to
rise up and tell the world who he thinks he is,be something,and do
things.Had I taught them I would have put this thought into them too
as I have others who are not Melungeon.
     Someday,I believe Daughter of the Legend might be considered my best
novel.It's a woman's book. No woman I know who has read it hasn't
gone into a deep feeling for Deutsia Huntoon and even shed tears for her.
But I created Deutsia Huntoon and Dave Stoneking,they are my literary
children. They are mine.I will fight for them and defend them on
any and every occasion.You help me.
     At twentyfour you have good years and writing years ahead of you,You
are just a girl.You have hundreds of Melungeon stories to write.They
are all around you and don't be too selfconscious to write them.Goodluck
and thanks for your fine letter.Give your father my best wishes as one
who remembers him so well,so well...

                              Sincerely,

                                  Jesse Stuart

                              Jesse Stuart

Greenup, Ky,
Jan, 12th 1967

Dear Druanna Overly:

Thank you for your quick response on what went on in Sneedville and for your sending me this Clipping. I'm glad to have this Clipping.

One of my students, LEE Pennington, who has written a book on my Novels, Says, Daughter of the Legend is great. I wish you Could read his Chapter on this book. The title of his book is: The Dark Hills of JESSE Stuart (His Vision and His Symbolism.).

2

The book is limited to 500 Copies (all will sell quickly). David Brandenburg, 11982 Marwood Lane, Cincinnati, Ohio published this book.

I wrote Daughter of the Legend 1941 — It was published in 1965. I agree it should have been published sooner.

Since I couldn't be with the group meeting in Greedville, I sent a letter down there. I hope they do this play and make a theatre here. I would put Greedville on the Map

Sincerely,
Jesse Stuart

March 5th 1936
Taylor, Kentucky

To Drew B. Williams and wife:

My College
friends from Lincoln Memorial—
I send this book as a part
of me. I hope you like these
furrows, these Kentucky rocks,
birds, and people from
Kentucky and Tennessee—
my best regards to you
always.

Sincerely,
JESSE Stuart

Bibliography

Sources

"As Others See Him." *The Church on the Hill* (newsletter of the Presbyterian Church in Englewood Cliffs, New Jersey). January 1944.

Bell, Geraldine Hatfield. Vardy Oral Histories. Interviewed by DruAnna Overbay, Blountville TN, 19 August 1999.

Bell, George. *Vardy School Newspaper* article. Scrapbook of Vardy Principal Mossie Kate Overton, 1942–1945.

Bell, Josephine. *Vardy School Newspaper* article. Scrapbook of Vardy Principal Mossie Kate Overton, 1942–1945.

Bell, Mattie. *Vardy School Newspaper* article. Scrapbook of Vardy Principal Mossie Kate Overton, 1942–1945.

Callahan, Jim. *Lest We Forget: The Melungeon Colony of Newman's Ridge.* Johnson City TN: Overmountain Press, 2000.

Campbell, Mossie Kate Overton. Telephone interview by DruAnna Overbay, June 2003.

Collins, Boyd Ward. Personal letters.

Collins, Cleland. Vardy Oral Histories. Interviewed by Sally Collins and DruAnna Overbay. Morristown TN, 25 April 1999.

Collins, Eula Mullins. Vardy Oral Histories. Interviewed by Katie Doman. Baltimore, March 2002.

Collins, Noah. Vardy Community Presbyterian Church Records. Vardy TN, 1902–1919.

Collins, Oakey Hendrix. Vardy Oral Histories. Interviewed by Sally Collins and DruAnna Overbay. Morristown TN, 25 April 1999.

Collins, Pearl. *Vardy School Newspaper* article. Scrapbook of Principal Mossie Kate Overton, 1942–1945.

Collins, Thomas. Vardy Oral Histories. Interviewed by Sally Collins. West Liberty KY, 21 June 2002.

Collins, W. C. Personal Comments and Correspondence to DruAnna Overbay, August 1996–August 2002.

_____. Vardy Oral Histories. Interviewed by Katie Doman. Sneedville TN, 7 August 2000.

Collins, William. *Vardy School Newspaper* article. Scrapbook of Principal Mossie Kate Overton, 1942–1945.

Cummins, Glessie Collins. Vardy School Alumni Questionnaire, 4 September 2004.

Davidson, Elizabeth Horton. Personal Correspondence to Macie Mullins, *Vardy Voice.* May 2002.

Davidson, Geraldine. *Vardy School Newspaper* article. Scrapbook of Principal Mossie Kate Overton, 1942–1945.

Doman, Katie. Submitted manuscript to *Windows on the Past.* 20 June 2002.

Elmore, Amelia Barr. "Family Portrait." *The Church on the Hill* (newsletter of the Presbyterian Church in Englewood Cliffs, New Jersey). January 1943.

Franz, Audrey Mullins. Vardy Oral Histories. Interviewed by Katie Doman. Baltimore, March 2000.

Gibson, Leonard. "Remembering Vardy School." Manuscript given to Katie Doman, interviewer. Baltimore, 6 March 2000.

Gibson, Willie Jack. *Vardy School Newspaper Article*. Scrapbook of Principal Mossie Kate Overton, 1942–1945.

Goins, Jack Harold. *Melungeons and Other Pioneer Families*. S.n., 2000.

Grohse, Willie 0. *VCHS Board Meeting Minutes*. July 1998.

Grohse, W. P., Jr. "A Brief History of Vardy Community, Hancock County." Manuscript given to Alyce and Drew Williams. Williams Family Collection.

_____. Vardy Historian's personal notes (1931–1977). Mattie Mae Grohse Collection.

Horton, Billie Mullins. Vardy Oral Histories. Interviewed by Katie Doman. Sneedville TN, 9 August 2000.

Horton, Claribel Miser. Vardy Oral Histories. Interviewed by DruAnna Overbay. Seymour IN, August 1999.

"How Vardy Converts Muscle into Books." *The Church on the Hill* (newsletter of the Presbyterian Church in Englewood Cliffs, New Jersey). November 1943.

"How Vardy Yielded to the Gospel." *The Continent*. 1916.

"Information, Please." *The Church on the Hill* (newsletter of the Presbyterian Church in Englewood Cliffs, New Jersey). January 1943.

Johnson, Etta Jane. *Vardy School Newspaper* article. Scrapbook of Principal Mossie Kate Overton, 1942–1945.

Leonard, Chester F. "Helping a Community Help Itself." *The Presbyterian Advance*. 18 October 1928.

_____. "How We Use Slides." *Church Management*. December 1939.

_____. Personal Correspondence to Drew Williams. 1946–1952.

_____. "Annual Reports." Vardy Community Presbyterian Church Records, 1929–1945.

Leonard, Josephine. Personal Correspondence to David F. Swartz. 9 July 1952 and June 1971.

_____. "Vardy's First Christmas Decorations." Given to Margaret Williams Nevels, June 1971.

Martin, James D. "McCormick Alumnus: C. F. Leonard." *McCormick Speaking*. November 1947.

Miser, Cecil. *Vardy School Newspaper* article. Scrapbook of Principal Mossie Kate Overton, 1942–1945.

Moore, Robert. Vardy Oral Histories. Interviewed by DruAnna Overbay. Talbott TN, 13 July 2002.

Muhlbauer, Ruth Jenkins. Telephone interviews by DruAnna Overbay. July 2002.

_____. Telephone interviews by DruAnna Overbay. January 2005.

————. Vardy Oral Histories. Interviewed by Katie Doman. Baltimore, March 2000, and Vardy Reunion, September 2000.

Mullins, Barbara. *Vardy School Newspaper* article. Scrapbook of Principal Mossie Kate Overton, 1942–1945.

Mullins, Betty. *Vardy School Newspaper* article. Scrapbook of Principal Mossie Kate Overton, 1942–1945.

Mullins, Esther. *Vardy School Newspaper* article. Scrapbook of Principal Mossie Kate Overton, 1942–1945.

Mullins, Jesse. *Vardy School Newspaper* article. Scrapbook of Principal Mossie Kate Overton, 1942–1945.

Mullins, R. C. Vardy Oral Histories. Interviewed by DruAnna Overbay. Morristown TN, 15 June 2002.

————. "My Hard Candy Christmas." As told to Macie Mullins. Morristown TN, October 1999.

Nevels, Margaret Williams. "Remembering Vardy." Manuscript given to DruAnna Overbay, interviewer. 12 July 2000.

————. "Remembering Miss Rankin and Mrs. Leonard." E-mail to DruAnna Overbay, 16 August 2002.

Overbay, DruAnna Williams. Personal Notes. 1963–2002.

Overbay, DruAnna, Claude Collins, Charles Sizemore, Troy Williams, and R. C. Mullins. "The Vardy School." *Panel at Fourth Union: A Melungeon Gathering*. CD recording by Wayne Winkler of WETS-FM, Kingsport TN, MHA, 21 June 2002.

Rhea, Johnnie Gibson. Vardy Oral Histories. Interviewed by Katie Doman. Sneedville TN, 10 August 2000.

Sexton, Mae Williams. Vardy Oral Histories. Interviewed by Troy Williams. Laurel MD, 28 September 1999.

Sizemore, Charles. Vardy Oral Histories. Interviewed by Theresa Burchette. Vardy Church, Sneedville TN, February 2000.

"Survey of Vardy Presbyterian Church." Vardy Community Presbyterian Church Records. 1902–1977.

Swartz, David F. "They Came. They Stayed." Manuscript given to Vardy Community Historical Society, June 2001.

————— Vardy Oral Histories. Interviewed by DruAnna Overbay. Boone NC, 5 June 1999.

"Vardy Dedicates Service Flag." *The Church on the Hill* (newsletter of the Presbyterian Church in Englewood Cliffs, New Jersey). November 1943.

"Vardy School News." *Vardy School Newspaper* article. Scrapbook of Principal Mossie Kate Overton, 1942–1945.

Williams, Alyce Horton. "Remembering My Life." Manuscript given to DruAnna Overbay.

Williams, Charlotte. *Vardy School Newspaper* article. Scrapbook of Principal Mossie Kate Overton, 1942–1945.

Williams, Daniel H. Vardy Oral Histories. Interviewed by DruAnna Overbay. Knoxville TN, 15 June 2002.

_____ *Vardy School Newspaper* article. Scrapbook of Principal Mossie Kate Overton, 1942–1945.

Williams, Drew B. Vardy Community Presbyterian Church Records, 1935–1957.

Williams, Lewis Alder. "The Mail Carrier—Lewis Alder." *Vardy Voice*. August 2002.

Williams, LLoyd. Vardy Oral Histories. Interviewed by Katie Doman. Baltimore MD, 8 March 2000.

Williams, Luigene. *Vardy School Newspaper* article. Scrapbook of Principal Mossie Kate Overton, 1942–1945.

Williams, Mae. *Vardy School Newspaper* article. Scrapbook of Principal Mossie Kate Overton, 1942–1945.

Williams, Troy L. Personal Comments to DruAnna Overbay 1996–2002.

_____. Vardy Oral Histories. Interviewed by Theresa Burchett. Vardy Church, Sneedville TN, March and April 2000.

Index